## ENDA WALSH

Enda Walsh was born in Dublin an.
include a radical adaptation of *A Christmas Carol* (Corcadorca,
1994), *The Ginger Ale Boy* (Corcadorca, 1995), *Disco Pigs*
(Corcadorca, 1996, then Traverse Theatre, Edinburgh, 1997; winner
of the 1997 Stewart Parker Award and the 1997 George Devine
Award), *Sucking Dublin* (Abbey Theatre, Dublin, 1997), *Misterman*
(Corcadorca, 1999; Galway Arts Festival and St Ann's Warehouse,
New York, 2011, and National Theatre, 2012), *bedbound* (The New
Theatre, Dublin, 2000, then Traverse Theatre, 2001, and Royal
Court Theatre Upstairs, 2002), two short plays, *How These Men
Talk* (Zürich Schauspielhaus, 2004) and *Lynndie's Gotta Gun* for
Artistas Unidos (Lisbon's National Theatre, 2005), *The Small
Things* (Paines Plough at the Menier Chocolate Factory, London,
2005), *Chatroom* (National Theatre, 2005), *The Walworth Farce*
(Druid Theatre, Galway, 2006, then Traverse Theatre, 2007, and
National Theatre, 2008; winner of Fringe First Award, 2007), *The
New Electric Ballroom* (Kammerspiele, Munich, 2005, then Druid
Theatre, Galway, and Traverse Theatre, 2008; winner of Theater
Heute's Best Foreign Play, 2005, Fringe First Award, 2008, Best
New Play, Irish Times Theatre Awards, 2008), *Delirium*, an
adaptation of Dostoevsky's *The Brothers Karamazov* (for Theatre
O, Abbey Theatre and Barbican, 2008), *My Friend Duplicity*
(Edinburgh Festival Fringe, 2010), *Penelope* (Traverse Theatre,
2010, then Hampstead Theatre, 2011; winner of Fringe First Award,
2010), *Room 303* (an installation for Galway International Arts
Festival, 2014), *Ballyturk* (Galways International Arts Festival and
National Theatre, 2014). *Disco Pigs* and *bedbound* have been
translated into eighteen languages and have had productions
throughout Europe.

His plays for radio include *Four Big Days in the Life of Dessie
Banks* for RTÉ, which won the IPA Radio Drama Award, and *The
Monotonous Life of Little Miss P* for the BBC, which was
commended at the Grand Prix, Berlin. His 2008 biopic *Hunger* told
the story of the final days of IRA hunger striker Bobby Sands and
won awards including the Caméra d'Or at the Cannes Film Festival
and the Heartbeat Award at the Dinard International Film Festival.
It was nominated for seven BIFAs (including Best Screenplay), six
British Film and Television Awards (including Best Screenplay and
Best Independent Film) and BAFTA's Outstanding British Film
Award 2009.

ENDA WALSH

# Plays: Two

The Walworth Farce
The New Electric Ballroom
Penelope
My Friend Duplicity
Room 303
Ballyturk

*with a Foreword by the author*

NICK HERN BOOKS
London
www.nickhernbooks.co.uk

**A Nick Hern Book**

*Enda Walsh Plays: Two* first published in Great Britain as a paperback original in 2014 by Nick Hern Books Limited, The Glasshouse, 49a Goldhawk Road, London W12 8QP

*Room 303* first published in an earlier version in *Sixty-Six Books: 21st-century writers speak to the King James Bible* by Oberon Books, 2011

Cover image © Patrick Redmond

Designed and typeset by Nick Hern Books, London
Printed in Great Britain by Mimeo Ltd, Huntingdon, Cambridgeshire
PE29 6XX

ISBN    978 1 84842 422 7

# Contents

## Foreword

When we moved from Cork to London – about ten years ago now – we rented a house off the Old Kent Road. My wife Jo got a job at the *Independent* newspaper and I acquisitioned a box bedroom to write some plays in. I didn't know many people in London back then – and those I first got to know were working the cash registers in my local Tesco.

On the bus on the way into the city I would pass the roundabout on the Elephant and Castle. Inevitably the bus would stop in heavy traffic and I remember deciding I would write a play about that very spot and about that feeling of being trapped and churned by your environment.

The play – *The Walworth Farce* – formed itself as a high-octane farce, which was a real surprise as we have no history of that style of performance back in Ireland. I had that image of farce seeping out of the West End and tunnelling under the Thames and finding its way to a tower block – and into the unfortunate lives of these Irishmen who really should be building Britain.

The play quickly wrote in three weeks and as I was writing it I had already decided to write a companion piece called *The New Electric Ballroom*. Both plays I think of as very Irish – plays about a shared family story where a person visiting will somehow force the truth out of that uncertain history. *The New Electric Ballroom* was quieter – more elegiac – but again it became about the pressures of the environment on these isolated characters.

Both plays kickstarted my collaboration with Mikel Murfi. I was a huge fan of his work as a director and actor when I saw him in Dublin. He signed up to direct *The Walworth Farce* for Druid in Ireland, came over to London where we sat in my attic drinking tea and performing the Farce to one another – our combined energy could have powered a small city. Mikel went on to perform as Patsy in *The New Electric Ballroom* – both plays toured around the world for a few years and their dark twisting of nostalgia seemed to strike a chord – particularly in America.

I'm always surprised how my British contemporaries often write plays directly about the world around them – like theatre is there to dramatise what we see in the news or talk about at dinner parties. It's very peculiar and at its best it can be powerful and feel vital, I suppose. My one attempt to talk specifically about 'something that was actually happening' was in the play *Penelope*.

When the crash in 2008 decimated the fantasy that Ireland had created for itself, a German theatre in Oberhausen had already approached me and four other European playwrights to each take a section of the *Odyssey* to adapt. I was reading a lot about Irish bankers and financiers who were either killing themselves or being publicly vilified. I decided to write a play about Penelope's suitors as they await their collective murder. It became part-situation-comedy, part-existential-scratching – scored by Herb Alpert. Not exactly social commentary then but it was what it was. Mikel directed the English-language premiere and the work I could tell was becoming more visual – a little more abstracted than before.

Two short plays followed – *My Friend Duplicity* and *Room 303*. Together – and I can only see it now – the themes of both plays had an effect on the final 'large' play in this volume – *Ballyturk*.

While the early plays – in the previous collection – were driven by language, I think – this collection is concerned more with a play's shape. *The Walworth Farce* locked the characters in a very mathematical form – shifting them about to the tight rhythms and rules of farce.

In *Ballyturk*, the play is guided by an outside force too. Like the characters, the play feels directionless and lost – thrown from one atmosphere to another. The question of what an audience takes home – what they experience – kept being asked. With *Ballyturk* we would tell a story – but more significantly we wanted an audience to experience form shifting radically.

Though I'm loath to define it for myself, the work in recent years is changing in other ways too. The process remains the same from when I was in my early twenties – I trust my instincts – the play will find its own shape, its own way.

They are written to be performed of course – but I do hope there's something in these plays for a reader too.

Thanks.

*Enda Walsh, 2014*

# THE WALWORTH FARCE

*The Walworth Farce* was first performed by Druid Theatre
Company at the Town Hall Theatre, Galway, on 20 March 2006.
The cast was as follows:

| | |
|---|---|
| DINNY | Denis Conway |
| SEAN | Aaron Monaghan |
| BLAKE | Garrett Lombard |
| HAYLEY | Syan Blake |

| | |
|---|---|
| *Director* | Mikel Murfi |
| *Designer* | Sabine Dargent |
| *Lighting Designer* | Paul Keogan |

The production subsequently toured to the Everyman Palace
Theatre, Cork, and the Helix, Dublin.

The play was revived at the Traverse Theatre, Edinburgh, on
3 August 2007, with the following cast:

| | |
|---|---|
| DINNY | Denis Conway |
| SEAN | Tadhg Murphy |
| BLAKE | Garrett Lombard |
| HAYLEY | Natalie Best |

The play received its London premiere at the National Theatre
in September 2008, with Mercy Ojelade playing the role of
Hayley.

4

**Characters**
*in order of appearance*

DINNY, *fifty, Irish accent*

BLAKE, *twenty-five, Irish accent*

SEAN, *twenty-four, Irish accent*

HAYLEY, *twenty-four, South London accent*

## ACT ONE

*The set is three square spaces. Essentially a living room at its centre, a kitchen to stage left and a bedroom to stage right.*

*Much of the plasterboard has been removed from the walls and what remains are the wooden frames beneath.*

*The two doors on the wall leading into the kitchen and the two doors leading into the bedroom on the other wall have been removed.*

*The back wall shows the front door leading into this flat.*

*There are two wardrobes at the back made from the plaster-board. One on the left and one on the right of the front door.*

*The decor is at best drab. Everything worn and colourless and stuck in the 1970s.*

*There is an armchair and a small coffee table in the sitting room with six cans of Harp on it. The kitchen is fitted and very messy. The bedroom has two single beds on top of each other made to look like bunk beds.*

*We're in a council flat on the Walworth Road, South London.*

*As the lights go up we see a man sitting in the armchair. This is the father, DINNY. He wears a bad brown yellowing wig on his head, a tight ill-fitting suit that makes him look clownish. He has a jet black bushy moustache. He's holding a small biscuit tin.*

*On a side table next to him he presses the button of an old tape recorder. 'An Irish Lullaby' begins to play. Slowly he opens the biscuit tin. He looks inside, smiles and smells the contents. He closes it and places it under the armchair. He begins to polish his shoes with a tin of brown polish.*

*His son BLAKE stands in his vest and underpants and irons something on a coffin-shaped cardboard box in the bedroom.*

BLAKE's *brother* SEAN *stands in the kitchen. He wears a woollen hat. He takes it off and places it in the pocket of his jacket. His hair has been shaved so that he looks as if he's badly balding.*

*He goes to the table where he looks into a Tesco bag. His expression suddenly shocked. He takes out an extremely large salami sausage. He goes to the oven and flings the sausage inside, closing the door. With trepidation he returns to the Tesco bag, reaches in and takes out a packet of Ryvita crackers. Again he's shook.*

DINNY *enters the kitchen carrying the tape recorder and* SEAN *quickly hides the Ryvita behind his back.* DINNY *pours himself a glass of water and gargles for a bit.* SEAN *watches him.* DINNY *spits it back in the sink, turns and exits the kitchen and back into the sitting room.*

DINNY *places the tape recorder on the side table and starts to do little physical jerks. He's exercising.*

BLAKE *is putting on what he was ironing. A floral skirt. He puts the iron under the bed and takes up a freshly ironed colourful blouse. He smells it. It's not the best. He sprays it with some Mister Sheen. He smells it again and puts it on. From under the bed he takes an old lamp with an orange floral shade. He slings it off a hook that hangs from the ceiling and turns it on. The bedroom is thrown into a new light.*

SEAN *meanwhile is making Ryvita sandwiches in the kitchen with spreadable cheese he's taken from a tiny fridge.*

DINNY *stops exercising. He takes off his wig and we can see some Velcro tape running on top of his head which obviously keeps on the wig. He takes a comb out and gives the wig a quick once over.*

BLAKE *puts on a woman's black permed wig. He picks up the cardboard coffin and exits the bedroom and into the sitting room and stands waiting.*

SEAN *sticks a bad fake moustache on (à la Magnum P.I.), dons a tight cream sports jacket which he buttons up and exits the kitchen.* BLAKE *hands him the coffin and enters one of the wardrobes.*

SEAN *stands holding the coffin on his shoulders by the front door and waits for his father.*

DINNY *sticks his wig back on. He goes to the wall and takes a small golden trophy off a shelf. He reverentially kisses it before carefully replacing it. He blesses himself.*

*He takes a deep breath and exhales sharply. He's ready.*

DINNY *holds the other end of the coffin with* SEAN. *He reaches to the light switch on the back wall and switches off the light in the sitting room as 'An Irish Lullaby' comes to an end.*

*The room is thrown into darkness and silence.* DINNY *immediately turns the light back on.*

DINNY. She was our mother, Paddy –

*Suddenly the tape recorder blasts out the Irish traditional song 'A Nation Once Again'.*

*The two of them startled.*

Shite!

DINNY *turns off the tape recorder. Again he takes a deep breath and exhales sharply. He then reaches back to the light switch and turns the lights off again. He immediately turns them back on.*

*The Farce begins. The three speak in Cork City accents. The performance style resembles The Three Stooges.*

She was our mother, Paddy, and she treated us well.

SEAN AS PADDY. It was a happy outcome, Dinny, even if it was her funeral.

DINNY. To see her little smiling face all done up in that make-up, looking like a movie star, wasn't she?

SEAN AS PADDY. A little miracle how her head was recreated when you think of the wallop that horse gave her. Hit by a dead horse. Who would have believed it?

DINNY. As the priest said, Paddy... only the good Lord knows of our final curtain.

SEAN AS PADDY. I fear He does.

DINNY. It was God's will to send a massive dead stallion careering over a hedge.

SEAN AS PADDY. Yes.

DINNY. God's will to send it crashing on top our sweet mother's tiny body as she innocently picked gooseberries for her own consumption on that quiet country road. Whatever way you look at it, Paddy, religion's awful cruel.

SEAN AS PADDY. Is that cans of beer over there?

DINNY. It is, they are.

SEAN AS PADDY. It's just she's getting awful heavy…

DINNY. Stick her in the dining room there, Paddy. Don't want my two little boys having nightmares.

SEAN *and* DINNY *take the coffin into the bedroom.*

SEAN AS PADDY. So this is your place, Dinny?

DINNY. Built with my own hands… figuratively speaking of course. Not much call for building work in my line of work.

BLAKE AS MAUREEN *enters from the wardrobe.*

BLAKE AS MAUREEN. You want me to fix the sandwiches, Dinny?

DINNY. Go heavy on the cheese spread, sweetheart. You know how I like my sandwiches, Maureen love.

BLAKE AS MAUREEN. Where's the kitchen?

DINNY *secretly and aggressively points over to where it is.*

BLAKE AS MAUREEN *quickly enters the kitchen. He immediately takes off his wig and puts on a new red-haired permed wig and re-enters the wardrobe.*

SEAN AS PADDY. What is it you do again, Dinny?

DINNY. Brain surgery, Paddy.

SEAN AS PADDY. And to think you were thrown out of school at fifteen.

DINNY. Ireland's a terrible hole and you'll get no argument from me… but I'll say this about it… it gives fools a fighting chance.

SEAN AS PADDY. Fair play.

DINNY. Not like London, Paddy?

SEAN AS PADDY. London's a tough old nut. For a while I was working the sites but London's all grown up now and not much building for fellas like me. Truth is I haven't worked for six years, Dinny.

DINNY. You've flat feet of course.

SEAN AS PADDY. The flat feet are only half of it, there's more. Being a man of medicine you may have heard of my condition.

DINNY. You've got a condition?

SEAN AS PADDY. A critical condition.

DINNY. Proceed.

SEAN AS PADDY. I'm getting pains in my hole, Dinny.

DINNY (*carefully*). Yes.

SEAN AS PADDY. Remember as a little boy that big railing I impaled myself on… pierced my back?

DINNY. Oh that hole!

SEAN AS PADDY. It just missed the heart, didn't it. When I get too excited, Dinny, I fall over…

DINNY. Do ya?

SEAN AS PADDY. I do! Blood stops racing to the head… I collapse.

DINNY. Collapse!? Good Lord!

SEAN AS PADDY. Doctor says one day I might never wake up. Thought it might happen to me today what with Mammy and everything.

DINNY. You had a pain in your hole today?

SEAN AS PADDY. A shocking pain in my hole, Dinny.

DINNY. Well, you listen to me, little brother. I wasn't always there for you in the past.

SEAN AS PADDY. You were never there for me.

DINNY. That's right, you're right. But in the future. If there's anything you want, if that hole of yours is keeping you awake at night just pick up the telephone and give us a call.

*Enter* BLAKE AS VERA *from the wardrobe.*

BLAKE AS VERA. Those two boys of yours are terrorising a copper outside.

DINNY. The little feckers. Sort that out for us, Paddy.

SEAN AS PADDY *runs and disappears into the wardrobe closing the door behind him.*

BLAKE AS VERA. Well, haven't you done well for yourself!? Beautiful leather couch, lovely little ornaments. Nice shag carpet. That seen any action has it?

DINNY. Now a gentleman wouldn't say, Vera.

BLAKE AS VERA. He wouldn't but you would.

DINNY *and* BLAKE AS VERA *laugh.*

DINNY (*laughing*). Oh very good, very good!

BLAKE AS VERA. How'd you make the big leap from painting and decorating to brain surgery?

DINNY. Oh you might well ask that question, Vera love.

BLAKE AS VERA. I just did, Denis.

*A pause.*

DINNY. One day…

BLAKE AS VERA. Yes?

DINNY *really has to think hard about this.*

DINNY.… a few years ago… I was busy applying some paint to a client's wall. Now she was a woman who was forever complaining about headaches and such like. 'Denis,' she would say, 'I have such a terrible pounding in the head.' Well, the poor dear fell in front of me and cracked her head wide open. And there I was looking at my first brain. (*Easier now.*) Now I liken the brain to a walnut, Vera. Larger obviously and not the class of thing you'd hand out to kiddies at Hallowe'en... but a walnut all the same. She was still breathing so I had to act fast. Now Coca-Cola, which I had on my person for its thirst-quenching properties, is also a terrific... terrific preservative. Her head took two litres of Coca-Cola and a roll of masking tape to bind her right back up. The doctors said I saved her life because of my quick thinking, suggested to me a night course in basic brain surgery as I obviously had the knack for it and two years later... here I am!

BLAKE AS VERA (*she's not convinced*). That's quite a story.

DINNY. It certainly is.

> SEAN *re-enters from the wardrobe as his seven-year-old self.*

SEAN. All right we play in the back garden, Dad?

DINNY. Yes, Sean. Where's Blake?

BLAKE. Here, Dad.

DINNY. I want you to stay out there for the afternoon and look after your little brother, all right, Blake?!

BLAKE (*in awe*). This place is beautiful.

DINNY (*growling*). Outside outside!

> BLAKE *and* SEAN *run and enter a wardrobe.*

> DINNY *looks very agitated.*

> BLAKE AS VERA *and* SEAN AS PADDY *re-enter.*

SEAN AS PADDY. The little devils.

DINNY. Copper, all right?

SEAN AS PADDY. He was crying a little bit.

DINNY. They're feisty boys, them! Take after their old man.

SEAN AS PADDY. Little tearaways you mean.

DINNY. Tearaways! Not at all.

BLAKE AS VERA. The way they acted in mass.

DINNY. Giddy that's all.

BLAKE AS VERA. They set fire to a nun, Dinny.

DINNY. In fairness, they didn't know it was a nun. She frightened the life out of them, that's all.

BLAKE AS VERA. She was in a terrible state.

DINNY. Arrah she was put out wasn't she… eventually.

SEAN AS PADDY. You shouldn't have given them those Mars Bars earlier.

BLAKE AS VERA. Church is no place for Mars Bars, Dinny.

BLAKE *enters the kitchen and changes into* MAUREEN's *wig*.

DINNY. No place is no place for Mars Bars, Vera. The fact is the Mars Bar's like eating shit on a stick. Worse… sure doesn't it rot your teeth.

BLAKE AS MAUREEN *re-enters with Ryvita sandwiches on a plate*.

(*Announcing*.) Ahh sandwiches, great stuff, Maureen! My favourites aren't they?

SEAN *looks very nervous*.

BLAKE AS MAUREEN. Spreadable cheddar, Dinny…

DINNY *freezes when he sees them*.

DINNY. What's this?

BLAKE (*as himself*). Sandwiches, Dad.

DINNY. Ryvita sandwiches?

SEAN. There was no sliced pan in Tesco, Dad.

DINNY. Supermarket, isn't it?

SEAN. I know but…

DINNY. Didn't you go?

SEAN. I did, Dad.

DINNY. You didn't go.

SEAN. I did.

DINNY. Don't answer me back or I'll thump ya!

BLAKE. Maybe we –

DINNY. Shut up, you! The story calls for sliced pan bread, doesn't it?

SEAN. I know but –

DINNY. The story doesn't work if we don't have the facts and Ryvitas aren't the facts… they're not close to the facts. A batched loaf is close to the facts, a bread roll is closer still but a Ryvita?… A Ryvita's just taking the piss, Sean. A Ryvita's a great leap of the imagination.

BLAKE. It's the right cheese.

DINNY. Feck the cheese! It's sticking out like a sore thumb. Your mother would never make crispy sandwiches, would she? You two little boys playing out in the garden out there… you'll not be happy with Ryvita!

SEAN. I can go back to Tesco if you want.

DINNY. Ah forget about it. And another thing, don't be cutting corners, you!

SEAN. How'd you mean?

DINNY. 'London's a tough old nut. For a while I was working the sites but London's all grown up now and not much building for fellas like me.' Then what, then what?

SEAN. Truth is I haven't worked for six years…

DINNY. 'The truth be told the Irishman is not the master builder of yesteryear. That title belongs to the men of Eastern Europe. Built like buses they are. Feet like double beds. The truth is I haven't worked for six years, Dinny.'

SEAN. That's a new line, Dad.

DINNY. So?

SEAN. You want me to use it?

DINNY. Getting lazy on me?

SEAN. No, Dad.

DINNY. Sloppy, Sean.

SEAN. Sorry, Dad.

DINNY. You wanna get your act together. There'll be no chance of the actin' trophy gathering dust on your shelf if you don't pull up them socks, boy.

SEAN. Right, Dad.

DINNY (*pointing to the trophy*). The acting trophy, Sean!

SEAN. Yes, Dad.

DINNY. Acting trophy!

SEAN. I know, Dad.

DINNY. Blake, make your entrance.

   BLAKE *turns back into the kitchen. He sighs.*

BLAKE (*to himself*). Shite.

DINNY (*to* SEAN). We'll talk about this later, right?!

SEAN. All right, Dad.

   BLAKE AS MAUREEN *re-enters with the sandwiches.*

DINNY. Ahh sandwiches, great stuff! My favourites aren't they, Maureen?

BLAKE AS MAUREEN. Spreadable cheddar, Dinny.

DINNY. Ohh lovely! Rich and creamy.

   *He bites into the Ryvita sandwich but it crumbles all over the place. He grimaces and looks like he's about to explode but* SEAN *quickly continues the performance.*

SEAN AS PADDY. Terrible shock going all the way to the cemetery and not being able to stick Mammy in the ground.

DINNY. A disgrace.

SEAN AS PADDY. Whoever heard of a gravedigger without a digger. Like a postman without post, a brickie without bricks, a shopkeeper without a shop, a cook without a cooker, a footballer without a foot, a bus driver without a bus, a fishmonger without a fish –

BLAKE AS VERA (*stopping him*). Paddy!

SEAN AS PADDY. Awful though. You had every right to hit that gravedigger as we left for home, Dinny.

DINNY. Couldn't get up much speed in that hearse though.

SEAN AS PADDY. No.

DINNY. Still… I managed to reverse and have another pop off the little fecker. (*Laughs a little.*)

SEAN AS PADDY. Christ it's great to be back with the big brother! The brain surgeon living in the gaff on the hill overlooking Cork City in all its finery.

DINNY. And what news of London Town, Paddy? This Walworth Road off the Elephant and Castle, paint me a picture of this boulevard and its surrounding environs.

SEAN AS PADDY *clears his throat.*

SEAN AS PADDY. On my palate is only grey, Dinny.

DINNY. Right.

SEAN AS PADDY. Grey and muck. For these are the two primary colours that make up much of the Elephant.

DINNY. I see.

SEAN AS PADDY. And as for the Castle… not so much a fortress, for a billion cars daily circle this grassy knoll known as 'the roundabout'.

DINNY. 'Daily traverse'!

SEAN AS PADDY. For a billion cars daily *traverse* this grassy knoll known as 'the roundabout'.

DINNY. Better.

SEAN AS PADDY. A million tiny bedsits there are. Large carbuncles sprouting out from the ground. Massive flats. Deadly, pitiful places that even the rats have abandoned, the cockroaches have done cockroaching and all that's left is London people.

DINNY. Jaynee.

SEAN AS PADDY. To sum it up in pure Cork parlance... the place is a hole.

BLAKE AS VERA. The lot of London is, Dinny.

DINNY. You do often read stories that they do eat their young over there, Paddy and Vera. So criminal and violent they are that Londoners like nothing more than skinning an Irishman halfway through his drink.

SEAN AS PADDY. Sacrilegious, boy. Sacrilegious. (*He knocks back his can of beer.*)

BLAKE AS VERA. And what news of Cork City, Dinny?

DINNY. Well, Vera, my love, there she is laid out in front of us.

SEAN AS PADDY. Aw beautiful.

DINNY. Laid out in all her finery.

BLAKE AS VERA (*wistfully*). Ah Cork.

DINNY. I often do stand here after a long day brain-surgeoning and just drink in this wonderful sight with a fine glass of red wine and a packet of those green Pringles. For I liken Cork City to a large jewel, Paddy and Vera.

SEAN AS PADDY. Do ya?

DINNY. I do. A jewel with the majestic River Lee ambling through it, chopping the diamond in two before making its way to murkier climes... towards the poisonous Irish Sea for example. Ah yes, Cork City. You could call it Ireland's jewel but you'd be A FUCKING IDIOT, BOY. FOR IT IS, REALLY AND TRULY, IRELAND'S TRUE CAPITAL CITY.

SEAN *and* BLAKE *applaud.*

SEAN AS PADDY. Oh well said, Dinny!

DINNY. The red and the white, Paddy! The blood and the bandage, little brother! Blood and the bandage!

BLAKE AS VERA. I'll help Maureen prepare the chicken.

BLAKE AS VERA *goes to the kitchen and opens the oven. He nearly falls back in horror. He slams it shut immediately.*

SEAN AS PADDY. And Dinny, tell me, tell me… would Mammy stand beside you and look at this very same view?

DINNY. She would, Paddy. She would. Me with my red wine, her standing with a pint of Beamish in her hand.

SEAN AS PADDY (*smiling*). Ah yes.

DINNY. A bottle of Harp in her other hand.

SEAN AS PADDY. That's right.

DINNY. A large glass of whiskey by the coffee table.

SEAN AS PADDY. That's her.

DINNY. And a can of Heineken in her coat pocket.

SEAN AS PADDY. She loved her drink.

DINNY (*with admiration*). You know when they pulled that horse off her, you could actually smell the whiskey from her blood. I mean, that's incredible, boy.

SEAN AS PADDY. And I always thought it would be the drink that would finally kill her.

DINNY. Well, it was in a way, Paddy. Those gooseberries she was gathering were for fermenting in a lethal vat of alcohol she called her 'Preservative'.

SEAN AS PADDY. Ohh the irony.

DINNY. I know, cruel, isn't it? (*Instructing him.*) 'So what about the will, Dinny?!'

SEAN AS PADDY. So what about the will, Dinny?

DINNY (*snaps*). Jesus, Sean, quicker! Quicker!

SEAN AS PADDY. Did she mention to you what might be in the will?

*DINNY takes a moment, furious that SEAN has messed up. The two boys tense. Suddenly:*

DINNY. The will, she did, Paddy! She gave me a hint a few weeks ago. But as custom will have it, the will must be read with the wives present.

SEAN AS PADDY (*eagerly calling*). Vera, love, the will!

DINNY (*just as eager and rubbing his hands*). Maureen, sweetheart, the reading of the will.

*BLAKE comes running from the kitchen wearing MAUREEN's wig and carrying VERA's wig.*

*The three enter the bedroom and surround the coffin.*

Read it loud and clear, Maureen.

*BLAKE takes the will from a sealed envelope and reads it.*

BLAKE AS MAUREEN. 'To my loving sons Denis and Patrick.'

SEAN AS PADDY. Nice touch.

BLAKE AS MAUREEN. 'I'm on the bus back home from the pub and fairly tanked up so here's the will. As your father would say, you two boys were the only family we ever had, you weren't much but we loved you… though we never got around to showing it on account of the terrible poverty we were under.'

DINNY. That's true.

BLAKE AS MAUREEN. 'But as you know the house you grew up in is now worth a few bob and can be carved up between the both of you.

DINNY *clears his throat.*

However, it's my wish that the son who is the most sensible, the most successful with his own money, the most balanced in his own life, should act as executor of the estate.

DINNY *has started to smile and nod to himself.*

That son will organise a small allowance to be paid monthly into his brother's account so that he doesn't piss it up a wall.

DINNY *fails to suppress his laughter.*

(*Quickly.*) A memorandum of the special gifts I want divided between family members is listed below. All the best in life. The bus is stopped so that's me off to the chipper. Mammy.'

DINNY (*erupting*). Well, that's clear as clear!

SEAN AS PADDY. How d'you mean?

DINNY. Take a look around you, Paddy. A far cry from Walworth Road and its deserting rats, aren't we?

SEAN AS PADDY. Suppose.

DINNY. She had mentioned to me she was worried the money wouldn't be handled sensibly what with our histories. She's looking for a steady hand, you see.

BLAKE AS VERA. He's lying, he's lying, Paddy!

SEAN AS PADDY (*looking at the will*). He's not, Vera! That's Mammy's will all right. You can smell the Bushmills off it.

DINNY. Fear not, little brother. As controller of the estate and your yearly allowance I'll make sure things are completely transparent.

SEAN AS PADDY. Monthly allowance.

DINNY. In the meantime we can keep ourselves happy with the personal gifts left in the memorandum by Mammy. Maureen, sweetheart.

BLAKE AS MAUREEN (*reading*). 'My deep fat fryer for my son Denis.'

DINNY (*triumphantly*). Yes!

BLAKE AS MAUREEN. 'And three cans of Harp for Patrick.'

SEAN AS PADDY. Ah Jesus.

DINNY (*laughing*). Three cans of Harp! You always were her favourite. You need a hand basting that chicken, Maureen!?

DINNY *and* BLAKE AS MAUREEN *leave the bedroom and walk across to the kitchen.*

(*Still laughing.*) Jesus but it's working like a dream.

BLAKE AS MAUREEN (*distracted*). This house is beautiful.

DINNY (*laughing*). A brain surgeon!? Can you believe it?! We'll fill them with the roast chicken and get them on the car ferry back to London. A monthly allowance? He's got two chances… none and…

BLAKE *pulls a baking tray out of the oven with the huge salami sausage on it. Seeing it:*

(*Snaps and screams.*) SEAN!

SEAN. Coming, Dad!

SEAN *comes running from the bedroom towards the kitchen.* DINNY *grabs a large frying pan.*

DINNY (*growls to himself*). A fecking sausage!?

SEAN *enters and immediately* DINNY *swings the frying pan across the back of* SEAN*'s head.* SEAN *hits the floor fast.*

*A long pause as* DINNY *and* BLAKE *look at* SEAN *on the floor.*

DINNY *takes a cup of water and gargles a little. He then spits it out on* SEAN*'s head.*

(*To* BLAKE, *calmly.*) Get him up and sort him out.

DINNY *goes back into the living room and sits in the armchair. He takes his wig off. He takes up a massive bottle of moisturising cream, squeezes some in his hand and aggressively applies it to his face and head.*

BLAKE *helps* SEAN *up.*

SEAN *sits at the table and* BLAKE *stands.*

*A long pause.*

*The two brothers talk in hushed tones.*

BLAKE. Are you okay?

SEAN. Yeah.

*A pause.*

BLAKE. What's with the shopping?

SEAN. I picked up the wrong bag in Tesco. (*A pause.*) It was a mistake.

BLAKE *looks in at* DINNY.

What's he doing?

BLAKE. Puttin' on his cream.

BLAKE *faces into the kitchen.*

*A long pause.*

SEAN. Something else happened to me, Blake.

BLAKE. Did someone try to get ya?

SEAN. No. No one ever does. You should come out with me the next time.

BLAKE *doesn't respond.*

*A pause.*

DINNY *is smelling the contents of the biscuit tin again.*

BLAKE. When we came here as little kids you could still smell Ireland from our jumpers.

SEAN (*distantly*). Yeah.

BLAKE. You could smell Mammy's cooking, couldn't you? It was roast chicken that last day and it was a lovely smell, hey Sean? And I think we might have come across on a boat… (*Prompting* SEAN, *smiling.*) Go on.

BLAKE *holds* SEAN*'s hand.*

SEAN (*continuing*). And despite the sea and wind, the smell of Mammy's cooking and that chicken was still stuck in the wool of our jumpers.

BLAKE. And I can't remember getting off a boat... but maybe we got a bus then to London, Sean, and still Mammy right around us.

SEAN. And Dad must have locked the door as soon as we were inside because the smell sort of stayed longer.

BLAKE. And for a while it stayed and we must have talked about the chicken smell and we must have missed Mammy, hey Sean?

SEAN. Yeah, we must have.

BLAKE. Dad all talk of Ireland, Sean. Everything's Ireland. His voice is stuck in Cork so it's impossible to forget what Cork is. (*A pause.*) This story we play is everything. (*A pause.*) Once upon a time my head was full of pictures of Granny's coffin and Mr and Mrs Cotter and Paddy and Vera and Bouncer the dog and all those busy pictures in our last day. (*Smiling.*) 'Cause you'd say Dad's words and they'd give you pictures, wouldn't they, Sean? And so many pictures in your head... Sure you wouldn't want for the outside world even if it was a good world! You could be happy. (*A pause.*) But all them pictures have stopped. I say his words and all I can see is the word. A lot of words piled on top of other words. There's no sense to my day 'cause the sense isn't important any more. No pictures. No dreams. Words only. (*A pause.*) All I've got is the memory of the roast chicken, Sean.

DINNY *enters the kitchen.*

DINNY. Explain the shopping to me then?

SEAN. A mistake, Dad.

DINNY. How a mistake?

SEAN. Someone tricked me with the wrong bag.

DINNY. Did they?

SEAN. Yes, Dad.

DINNY. Who?

SEAN. The girl at the cash register.

DINNY. Made fun of you, did she? Tricked you and then had a good laugh?

SEAN. She was a little bitch, Dad.

DINNY. She was a little bitch. And many more feckers out there, Sean, wanting to gobble you up.

SEAN. I can go back if you want.

DINNY. You're not enjoying going outside are you?

SEAN. Only if you want me to.

DINNY. Seems to me you might be enjoying it a little.

SEAN. No.

DINNY. Not like Blake here who knows he can't go out.

SEAN. I hate it too, Dad.

DINNY. Do you?

SEAN. I do.

DINNY. Are you lying to me about this girl that tricked you?

SEAN. No, Dad.

DINNY. 'Cause if you lie to me there'll be terrible trouble to pay.

SEAN. I know there will. There's no lying going on.

DINNY. Blake?

BLAKE. Yes, Dad.

DINNY. You're awful quiet.

BLAKE. Just keeping my energy. I know it's about to get real fast soon so just thinking things through again, that's all.

DINNY. Got your eyes on the actin' trophy, Blake? Such a prize.

BLAKE. Sure it's only you that gets to win it.

DINNY. But feck it, you're almost there, boy, almost.

BLAKE. Am I, Dad?

DINNY. You are. You've got the tough job playing the ladies, of course. (*Slight pause.*) Sort of nice playing Mammy though?

BLAKE. Yes, Dad.

DINNY. Christ she's a great woman, all right! A great woman! She'll be waiting in the kitchen back in Cork, lads! Waiting for her three men to walk back through the door.

BLAKE. When might that be, Dad? (*Slight pause.*) When?

DINNY *slowly inhales and announces loudly,*

DINNY. One day… ! One day!!

SEAN *races to the wardrobe.*

One day I'll buy a house just like this one, Maureen!

BLAKE *throws the sausage back in the oven and runs over and joins* SEAN *in the wardrobe.*

One day, by Jesus the Holy Christ, I'll live in a castle overlooking the banks of the lovely Lee. One day, mark my words! One day!

*Large thumping noise and* DINNY *is startled.*

By jaynee, who's this at the door?

SEAN *and* BLAKE *enter as Mr Cotter,* JACK, *and his brother-in-law* PETER *(both from Montenotte). They are carrying another cardboard coffin on their shoulders.*

BLAKE AS JACK. Watch the paintwork, Peter.

SEAN AS PETER. Sorry, Jack.

DINNY *freezes in the kitchen as he hears them.*

BLAKE AS JACK. I've just got a man in to do it for me actually. But by Jesus, what a day!

A gravedigger without a digger!? Have you ever heard of such shite.

SEAN AS PETER. Like a banker without a bank, a journalist without a journal, a painter without paint, a producer without produce, a publican without a pub, a zookeeper without a zoo…

BLAKE AS JACK. The list can go on, Peter, and we can just stand here with your dead father stuck in this box breaking my delicate little shoulders.

SEAN AS PETER. Well, it's your house, Jack, where do you want him?

BLAKE AS JACK. Stick him in the kitchen and out of my sight.

*As they go into the kitchen,* DINNY *runs out and across into the bedroom.*

BLAKE *and* SEAN *place the coffin down on the kitchen table.*

DINNY (*to himself*). By jaynee I wasn't expecting this at all! (*To* PADDY.) Back inside! Back inside! Look I'm sorry, Paddy, but they just called out of the blue. It wouldn't be appropriate to…

DINNY *has to wait for the two boys and is annoyed by this.*

(*Snapping.*) Move it, lads, for fuck sakes!

SEAN *exits the kitchen and runs over to the bedroom.* BLAKE *runs back to the wardrobe and enters it.*

SEAN AS PADDY. You're not going to introduce me to those men?

DINNY. It's business, Paddy.

SEAN AS PADDY. Brain-surgery business?

DINNY. That's right. Now I'll have to go out to my colleagues and talk to them, Paddy. Are you all right in here with these two lovely ladies?

SEAN AS PADDY. Three ladies, Dinny. Let's not forget Mammy just yet.

DINNY. You're right. (*Touching the coffin and sighing*.) Sorry, Paddy.

DINNY *turns away fast and exits the bedroom and into the sitting room at the same time as* BLAKE *enters from the wardrobe wearing a new woman's blonde permed wig. He plays the part of Mrs Cotter,* EILEEN.

BLAKE AS EILEEN (*upset*). Oh Denis!

DINNY. Yes Eileen.

BLAKE AS EILEEN. Where's the body, love?

DINNY. What?

BLAKE AS EILEEN. The coffin, Denis? The coffin.

DINNY. Well, let me explain first…

BLAKE AS EILEEN (*calls*). Peter!

DINNY (*to himself*). Shit shit!

BLAKE AS EILEEN *enters the kitchen and throws his arms around the coffin.*

DINNY *stands looking aghast at the coffin on the table.*

BLAKE AS EILEEN (*crying a little*). Did you know he slept in this box for two months before he… Like he had a premonition.

SEAN AS PETER. Really?

BLAKE AS EILEEN. He loved this box. And then to be struck down in his prime!

SEAN AS PETER. Daddy was ninety-six, Eileen.

BLAKE AS EILEEN. Take off the lid, I want to look at him.

DINNY *stands in the sitting room listening to their conversation. They look into the coffin.*

SEAN AS PETER. Well, there he is. (*Slight pause.*) Bits of him, anyway.

BLAKE AS EILEEN. He went the way he would have liked to though, didn't he, Peter?

SEAN AS PETER. He did.

BLAKE AS EILEEN. Off the coast of Kinsale travelling at 140 miles an hour. The wind in his hair, his little sailor's outfit on. Speeding fast 'til he hits that bloody sea lion. (*Starts to cry.*) The speedboat thrown into the air. The boat travelling through that field, is that right?

SEAN AS PETER. That's right.

BLAKE AS EILEEN. The horse coming from nowhere. He hits the horse at 100-mile an hour sending it careering over a hedge and onto a quiet country road…

DINNY *faints from the shock and hits the ground hard.*

Denis!?

SEAN AS PETER. Good God! Is he all right? Who is he anyway?

BLAKE AS EILEEN. Our painter-decorator.

DINNY *comes around.*

Are you all right, Denis pet?

DINNY (*distantly*). Mother…

BLAKE AS EILEEN. No, it's me, Eileen.

DINNY. Horse.

BLAKE AS EILEEN. No, I'm not a horse.

DINNY. Mother… killed… horse.

BLAKE AS EILEEN. No Denis, that's not right, love. Daddy killed horse.

SEAN AS PETER. And horse killed Daddy.

BLAKE AS EILEEN. Help him into the chair, Peter, quick.

DINNY *is 'unconscious' in the armchair as* SEAN AS PETER *and* BLAKE AS JACK *have a covert conversation.*

BLAKE AS JACK. Is Eileen…?

SEAN AS PETER. She's in the kitchen looking at Daddy again.

BLAKE AS JACK. Well, what a complete waste of time.

SEAN AS PETER. I know, I know!

BLAKE AS JACK. Filling him with drink, sticking him on that speedboat and to what end?!

SEAN AS PETER. Well, perhaps Eileen has his money? She could have taken it somewhere, couldn't she?

BLAKE AS JACK. I know my wife's face. She knew that your father kept his money in his house but this morning when we turned everything upside down and found nothing! Her face, Peter?! She was devastated, boy!

*He takes a can of beer from* SEAN AS PETER*'s hands and finishes it.*

SEAN AS PETER. Well, he'd hardly have gotten rid of it, would he?

DINNY *gets up from the armchair and goes to enter the bedroom as* SEAN AS PADDY *tries to exit the bedroom.*

DINNY. What the hell are you doing!?

SEAN AS PADDY. I have to go to the toilet.

DINNY. You can't.

SEAN AS PADDY. I'm bursting!

DINNY. You'll have to do it in there.

SEAN AS PADDY. It's a dining room!

DINNY. Out the window then.

SEAN AS PADDY. In front of the girls?

SEAN *exits the other door and appears in the living room as* PETER.

SEAN AS PETER. Are they your children out there?

DINNY. What?

SEAN AS PETER. In the garden. They're on the putting green outside.

BLAKE AS JACK *walking fast towards the wardrobe.*

BLAKE AS JACK. My putting green, the little shits!

*He enters the wardrobe.*

SEAN AS PETER. And I've seen some people inside the dining room.

DINNY *freezes.*

BLAKE AS EILEEN *re-enters the living room and heads for the kitchen.*

From the back garden. A man and two women, don't deny it now!

BLAKE AS EILEEN *pulls out the sausage in the pan.*

BLAKE AS EILEEN (*calling, confused*). Denis, love, what is this?

DINNY. Yes, Mrs Cotter.

BLAKE as EILEEN *brings the large sausage and pan inside to the living room.*

BLAKE AS EILEEN. Is this your chicken?

DINNY. I thought you might fancy a little bit of roast chicken after the funeral.

SEAN AS PETER. How did you know we were coming back? You couldn't have possibly known we were going to arrive back this afternoon. You've been eating Eileen and Jack's food, haven't you? (*He grabs the sausage.*) There's nothing you'd like more than having your three friends around, drinking someone else's alcohol and feeding yourselves with somebody else's chicken…

DINNY *screams. He grabs the large sausage and flings it against the wall. It disintegrates.*

*Long pause as* SEAN *and* BLAKE *brace themselves.*

DINNY (*quietly*). It's not working with the sausage. It's not right.

SEAN (*instinctively*). Is any of it?

*Immediately,* SEAN *regrets saying anything.* DINNY *grabs him by the hair.*

DINNY. What? Say it!

SEAN. Is any of this story real?

DINNY. Don't doubt me. We allow Mister Doubt into this flat and where would we be? Blake?

BLAKE. We'd be outside, Dad.

DINNY (*not liking* BLAKE's *tone*). Are you getting brave on me too?

BLAKE. I think I might want to go back to Ireland now.

DINNY. Do I not care for you both? The two little boys who followed me over, didn't I take you in and feed you? Little scraps all tired and hungry, wasn't it me who took you in?

BLAKE. Yes, Dad.

DINNY *grabs* BLAKE *by the ear and drags him into the sitting room.* SEAN *stands at the kitchen entrance looking at them.*

DINNY. And the sea, Blake. The sea, the sea, the sea, the sea, the sea…

BLAKE. Dad, don't!

DINNY's *delivery is focused and steady, he speaks it to* BLAKE.

DINNY. The sea it spits me out onto England. I stand on the shore with Ireland on my back and the tide pushing me across the land towards London. I run, Blake.

BLAKE. I know it, Dad.

DINNY. I run the same race a million Irishmen ran. But pockets full of new money and Paddy's keys in my hands with Walworth Road a final destination, a sure thing, a happy ever after. I run. I run right past the cars in the motorways, the trains in their tracks. I run fast towards London. Days and nights they merge into the one memory. Only the running has any matter. Countryside passing through me and a final farewell to the green. And no horizon of London, I see. No towers or flats or big gate to welcome Dinny. Just road signs and not grass under feet any more but hard grey now. The road signs steering me. Like a little rat caught in a drain. Pushing me further and further to its centre. But what centre? Me and my suit rolling down the motorway with buildings tighter on either side. And tighter and tighter still, Blake, and when they can't get any tighter, taller they grow. With each mile I run, higher they climb and smaller the dot. Higher the buildings and smaller me. I close my eyes from the size of this place. I stop. Stood still then. (*Long pause*.) The noise and running all stopped, Blake. And I'm stood on grass. I look down at my shoes all knackered… soles worn from the run. I catch my breath. I can hear my breathing. So it's all quiet, you see. Ssshhhhhh. (*A pause*.) I smell the roast chicken from my jumper, Blake. Your mother's kiss to me at the door and telling me, 'Leave now.' (*Slight pause*.) And I think of Paddy and Vera. Their little poisoned bodies piled up on the floor back in Mrs Cotter's house in Cork City. And then I think of me and Paddy as children back in the good old days. A day trip to Robert's Cove and Paddy runs into the sea, a big wave taking him, Dad lost in the pub and I wade in and pick the toddler up. It's only a little bit of water we stand in but Paddy's crying like a scared baba. I take him out and wrap him in Dad's towel. I keep him warm, you know. And I feel good when I think of me and the love I have for Paddy. I stand there looking at the green scabby grass of the roundabout and my knackered shoes. Fuck. (*A pause*.) And then what happened, Blake? What then, tell me?

BLAKE *continues, detached*.

BLAKE. And then it starts from the tiniest quiet thing. You can feel the little shakes up through the grass and up through your body now. Noises from the outside start filling you up. Loud car noises. Stood still with cars all wrapped around your head, stood in the middle of the Elephant and the Castle with Walworth Road right there in front of you. Walworth Road and Paddy and Vera's flat. Only the road to run and get inside, to get you safe. You run fast, Dad.

*His eyes suddenly fill with tears. He's terrified.*

And then the people. They come out from houses and shops and they're after you. Their skin, it falls to the ground and them bodies running you down and wanting to tear you to shreds. From the river they're coming. They come up from the ground. The concrete snaps open and the bodies are up fast. And they're all snapping teeth and grabbing hands they have. Run faster and faster until a thousand green windows reaching up into the sky and Paddy's flat right at the top and it's calling you. Take to the stairs with the other flats teeming out the bodies wanting to grab you down and get ya. The stairs and your speed. Further away from them you move as you climb higher and the flat higher still. Further away they fall as the flat still higher.

BLAKE *can't continue.*

DINNY. And then, Sean?

SEAN. At cloud height you are and looking over all of London with its bodies down below, its tighter-than-tight buildings, its chewed-up grey, them bad people calling you down. In Paddy and Vera's flat and you're looking over all them who want to gobble us up 'til we're no more. Inside and your heart begins to slow now that you have these safe walls. (*A pause.*) At the window and you're looking out past the end of Walworth Road, past where London stretches into the green countryside, past the green and over the sea to Ireland and to Cork and past the River Lee and high up into the estate and our little terraced house. (*Slight pause.*) And there's Mammy standing by the sink washing the dishes in the kitchen. From the window you can see all of this. In Paddy's flat and you're safe.

*Long pause.* DINNY *embraces* BLAKE.

DINNY. You believe that lie about that cash-register girl tricking Sean?

BLAKE *doesn't answer.* SEAN *looks on.* DINNY *looks at* SEAN *as he holds* BLAKE.

One lie leads to the next and pretty soon them bodies from outside be banging down our door and dragging you down below, Blake. You watch Sean for me, all right?

BLAKE *turns away and walks into the kitchen.*

SEAN *follows him inside.*

DINNY *sits down and begins to moisturise his head and face again.*

*When* BLAKE *enters the kitchen he goes straight to a drawer and takes out a large kitchen knife.*

SEAN *watches him.*

BLAKE *faces the sitting room ready to re-enter. The knife is meant for* DINNY.

BLAKE. Them bodies won't get us if we leave the flat, Sean?

SEAN. London's not the way he tells it.

BLAKE. You're sure of it? 'Cause I'm ready to finish it, Sean, but you're sure we won't be got by anyone outside?

SEAN. Well, today I spoke to someone.

BLAKE *turns to him.*

A girl in Tesco, Blake. Got all our food and paid her. She knows me 'cause I'm in at ten o'clock every morning getting the same food for the story. She says that she's seen where I live. Asks me what I do. I can't tell her the truth of what we do in here all day so I say that I'm a builder, though I'm no builder. She's talked about Ireland and how she's seen it on the telly, Blake. She talks about the funny colour of the grass and then the sea. I tell her that I like the sea but how I hadn't seen the sea in so long and she says, 'I'll take you to Brighton Beach and we can walk there.' She means it. She definitely means to take me to that place. So I leave sort of in a daze 'cause of the way she talked to me. I picked up the wrong shopping bag and didn't get out of the daze until I got back here and saw that fecking sausage. But her talking to me like that, Blake... even besides the great thing she said... her just talking so nice to me... it got me thinking more than ever... It's right that us two leave.

*A pause.* BLAKE*'s face hardens. He's not happy.*

BLAKE. You talked to someone outside?

SEAN. She's called Hayley.

*They suddenly hear 'A Nation Once Again' sung by Paddy Reilly blasting from the tape recorder.*

*SEAN walks through the living room through to the bedroom and takes up his position.*

*BLAKE violently slams the knife into the kitchen table.*

*He stares angrily in at SEAN.*

*He enters the living room as EILEEN and takes up his position.*

*Everything as it should be, DINNY turns off the music.*

BLAKE AS EILEEN. Can you explain this to me, Dinny?

DINNY. I can, Eileen, I can.

*SEAN AS PADDY enters the sitting room fast and races towards the wardrobe.*

SEAN AS PADDY. Sorry, Dinny, but the bladder's packed it in finally!

*He enters the wardrobe.*

BLAKE AS EILEEN. Who was that?

DINNY. My brother.

*BLAKE enters the bedroom and re-enters the sitting room as VERA and walks right across and into the kitchen and picks up a plate of Ryvita sandwiches.*

*SEAN AS PETER re-enters.*

SEAN AS PETER. So that's your brother in the toilet. Who was that?

DINNY. His wife.

SEAN AS PETER. And what is she doing here?

*BLAKE as VERA re-enters with the Ryvita sandwiches.*

BLAKE AS VERA. Just passing around these lovely sandwiches. I know you people could go a whole day without eating, just thinking those heady thoughts with no time for your stomachs. Didn't imagine that Dinny here would find himself in such illustrious company.

SEAN *goes back to the wardrobe*.

BLAKE AS EILEEN. And you made these sandwiches… ?

BLAKE AS VERA. Vera. No I didn't actually make them, no. It was Maureen.

BLAKE AS EILEEN. And who's she?

BLAKE AS VERA. Oh she's Dinny's wife!

BLAKE AS EILEEN. And is she… ?

BLAKE AS VERA. She's in the dining room, yeah. Sure I'll just get her for ya.

SEAN AS PETER *re-enters*.

SEAN AS PADDY. Well, thank God for that. Had an awful premonition that my hole would finally strike and I'd be lying prostrate on that lovely bathroom floor of yours. Well then!

DINNY. Eileen, this is Paddy the brother and my wife Maureen.

SEAN AS PADDY. Doctor.

BLAKE AS EILEEN. I beg your pardon?

SEAN AS PADDY. Is there a collective term for brain surgeons?

BLAKE AS EILEEN. I've no idea.

SEAN AS PADDY. You know Dinny here was thrown out of school when he was fifteen for smearing a school desk with…

DINNY. Thanks for that, Paddy.

SEAN AS PETER. Quite a gathering. With so many people helping surely your little job in the dining room is finished, Denis?

BLAKE AS VERA. What's there to do apart from sit around and grieve. The sandwiches are made, the chicken is cooking. We all just have to settle into a long evening of drinking. Drinking to life and toasting to death.

SEAN AS PETER. Well, that's very kind of you, Vera. It shows a beautiful character. Someone who can reach out to a stranger who's lost a parent.

BLAKE AS VERA (*covertly*). Can you see that?

SEAN AS PETER. Well, it's obvious.

BLAKE AS VERA. A stranger really?

SEAN AS PETER. Of course.

BLAKE AS VERA. You're right, you know. Do you think in eight years of marriage a person can end up a stranger with their own husband?

SEAN AS PETER. Well, that's an altogether different matter.

DINNY (*in mid-conversation*).… and Maureen knowing of this imminent gathering thought to prepare some finger food for us all.

BLAKE AS EILEEN. Maureen, that's very kind of you.

DINNY. Kind? Sure she lives for the kitchen!

BLAKE AS EILEEN. Even somebody else's kitchen, Maureen?

*A pause as* BLAKE AS MAUREEN *looks flustered.* DINNY *thrown.*

BLAKE AS MAUREEN. I'll get on with that chicken so!

DINNY. Great stuff, Maureen! Thanks, love.

BLAKE AS MAUREEN *walks into the kitchen, sees the open coffin and audibly gasps.*

DINNY *races into her.*

BLAKE AS MAUREEN (*whispering*). How did Mammy get over here?

DINNY. That's not Mammy. It's Mrs Cotter's father, look.

BLAKE AS MAUREEN (*looking inside*). What's he doing there?

DINNY. What do you think?! He's dead. Now stay put and cook, Maureen. Cook your little heart out! Get people's mouths full and they won't be able to speak, right.

DINNY *exits into the sitting room.*

BLAKE *exits into the stage right wardrobe.*

SEAN AS PADDY. Lovely people, Dinny! You'd imagine brain surgeons all stuffy. But nothing like it. She's lovely, Eileen! Said you were a great worker and that I could learn a lot from you… 'Though one brain surgeon in the family is enough, thank you very much, Eileen!' And look how that Peter fella's chatting up my Vera and getting close to her. Real charming bunch, aren't they? Christ it's shaping up into a lovely day!

BLAKE AS JACK *enters through the wardrobe.*

BLAKE AS JACK. Are these your two little boys, Denis!?

DINNY. Well, that depends, Mr Cotter…

BLAKE AS JACK. I walk out to the garden and they've got a neighbourhood child, Finbarr, pinned to the putting green. A great big bloody arm on him, Eileen. He's spread-eagled and knocked unconscious by these two little brats who are just about to do the unspeakable.

DINNY. Blake, explain this to me now?! Sean, come on.

SEAN. He was all by himself with his dog Bouncer and we thought it would be fun if he played with us.

BLAKE. Finbarr's in the scouts and came back with his tent so we could play soldiers.

SEAN. He told us about survival and how he was being trained to survive in the wild.

DINNY. What age is this boy?

BLAKE. Six.

DINNY. Carry on.

SEAN. So he's bragging, Dad. He's bragging about surviving in the wild, about pissing on snake bites when a snake does bite. And all this time he's unpacking his tent.

BLAKE. No tent in there, Dad. Just poles and pins.

SEAN. So I says that maybe he should be the tent. Maybe we should pin down Finbarr and stick a pole up his centre and keep cover under him.

BLAKE. We pin him down and he starts to cry like a baby and not the bush man he makes himself out to be. Sets his big dog on us. Now Sean's afraid of dogs, that's right, isn't it, Dad?

DINNY. He is, yeah.

BLAKE. So I pick up a pole and start on Bouncer to protect my little brother.

DINNY. Good man, Blake.

BLAKE. Give him a few whacks on the back and he's getting fierce angry.

SEAN. And all the time we're sort of dancing over 'Finbarr the tent' on the ground. When all of a sudden…

BLAKE. Snap!

SEAN. Terrible noise, Dad.

BLAKE. I look down and see Finbarr's little arm in Bouncer's mouth.

SEAN. He's only six so he's got every right to fall unconscious, Dad.

BLAKE. I take the tent pole and one last swipe, I fire it right up Bouncer's arse. He's away like a bat of hell with the pole still dangling out his rear end and here we are with Finbarr's bloody arm needing some serious attention.

SEAN. Well, all this talk of being out in the wild and surviving on the basics and what we did next just seemed liked the most natural.

BLAKE. Looking at his broken arm we decided to give it the snake bite treatment.

SEAN. So we pissed on him.

*A pause.*

DINNY *turns to 'the others' and shrugs his shoulders.*

DINNY. Fair play.

SEAN *enters the kitchen as* PETER.

BLAKE *enters the kitchen as* JACK.

BLAKE AS JACK (*furiously*). For Christ's sake, Peter. We shouldn't have bothered murdering this old shit.

*He grabs a can beer from* SEAN's *hand.*

SEAN AS PETER. Keep your voice down, Jack.

BLAKE AS JACK *drains the can of beer, much to* SEAN AS PETER's *annoyance.*

BLAKE AS JACK. For all his money your father's worthless to us. This coffin is worth more than him.

BLAKE AS JACK *pulls up the pillow.*

This ridiculous plump lining.

*He starts to bang the pillow off the coffin.*

Jesus the extravagance of the man. This silk bloody pillow with his initials on it for GOD'S SAKE!! I MEAN…

*Suddenly the pillow tears and Monopoly money is thrown in the air.*

*Suddenly the doorbell makes a continuous buzzing sound.*

*The three of them freeze.*

*The doorbell stops.*

*Instinctively,* BLAKE *grabs a kitchen knife to protect himself.*

BLAKE *and* SEAN *come out to the sitting room and look at the front door.*

*The doorbell sounds again.*

BLAKE *and* SEAN *look to their father. He points to* BLAKE *to open it.*

*With huge trepidation* BLAKE *walks towards the front door and begins to undo the many locks.*

*He then opens the door and steps way back as he holds the kitchen knife.*

*It's raining outside and standing in the rain is a twenty-four-year-old black woman holding a Tesco bag.*

*The three just stare at her.*

*This is* HAYLEY.

HAYLEY (*hesitantly*). Is Sean in? It's just he took the wrong shopping. This is his one.

*The three just look at her.*

HAYLEY *then recognises* SEAN.

Hey Sean! It's me, Hayley.

SEAN *wants to disappear. He looks at the floor.*

*She enters out of the rain.* BLAKE *moves back from her.*

*A pause.*

Hey.

DINNY. Is there a cooked chicken and sliced pan in there?

HAYLEY. Yeah. And two packets of pink wafers and... well what you usually get.

*A pause.*

DINNY. Can you cook?

HAYLEY. Why? Is this like *Ready Steady Cook* or something?! Only you don't look like Ainsley Harriott!

*She laughs.*

DINNY *just stares through her and waits for her to stop laughing.*

*She stops laughing.*

DINNY. Can you cook?

HAYLEY *a little awkward now.*

HAYLEY. Yeah.

HAYLEY *stands as the three just stare at her for a long time and the rain continues outside.*

*Loud guttural rhythmic music fades up and fills the stage and auditorium.*

*The music continues to build, the stage reverberating and unable to take its noise.*

*Blackout.*

*Silence.*

*Curtain Falls.*

*End of Act One.*

**ACT TWO**

*The curtain rises quickly.*

DINNY *stands in the centre of the sitting room staring towards the kitchen.*

BLAKE *stands near him also looking towards the kitchen where* HAYLEY *and* SEAN *are talking.*

*The nervous and talkative* HAYLEY *has her coat off and wears a Tesco uniform.*

SEAN*'s naturally very anxious about her being inside their flat.*

HAYLEY*'s staring into the coffin.*

HAYLEY. That's a big box. What are you using it for? Looks like a coffin.

SEAN. It's just cardboard.

HAYLEY. I tell you, after them stairs, I could climb right in there for a little nap. What we up here? Fourteen floors…

SEAN. Fifteen.

HAYLEY. Fifteen floors with no lift! You should get on to the Council. Took me ten minutes to get up. I'm a pretty fit girl. I play football down Burgess Park. Well try… I'm not bad… But the important thing is to keep healthy. Do you do anything to keep fit?

SEAN (*distracted*). I do a bit of running.

HAYLEY. You get a decent workout from those stairs. Every morning at ten o'clock, up with your shopping.

SEAN. Yeah.

DINNY *gestures to* BLAKE *to pay attention to* HAYLEY. BLAKE *stands by the kitchen entrance looking inside at her.*

HAYLEY. A creature of habit, aren't you? Oven-cooked chicken, white sliced bread, yeah?… Creamy milk, two packets of pink wafers, six cans of Harp and one cheesy spread. The other girls think you're an idiot but I was saying that there's a lot of sense to it. All the options that people have these days… it's all very confusing. If you're happy with your lifestyle and what you eat, why change?

*During the following exchange,* BLAKE *begins to mimic* HAYLEY*'s gestures, walk, stance. He's practising being her.*

*Unaware of this,* HAYLEY *suddenly notices the money on the kitchen floor.*

Is that Monopoly money?

SEAN. Yeah.

HAYLEY. Lively game was it? A bit messy in here. Is it just the three of you? Your brother and dad and you. No mother?

SEAN. She lives in Ireland.

HAYLEY. Divorced are they?

SEAN. No.

HAYLEY. Won't she come over? Doesn't she like London?

SEAN. I don't know.

HAYLEY. When you last see her?

SEAN. When I was five.

HAYLEY. Shut up! That's terrible. Five, really? Christ. Gotta get back and see her, Sean. Do you miss her?

SEAN. Yeah.

HAYLEY. Is she nice?

SEAN. She's a good cook.

HAYLEY. Aw you miss her cooking. How sweet. Why's your brother dressed like that?

SEAN. Like what?

HAYLEY. Like a woman. He's a transvestite, right?

SEAN. Ah what?

HAYLEY. He likes women's clothes.

SEAN. No it's a joke. He's just joking, that's all.

HAYLEY. I wouldn't mind if he was a transvestite.

SEAN. He's not.

HAYLEY. Well, I wouldn't mind if he was. It's a free world.

SEAN. He's a joker.

HAYLEY. He's a builder as well is he?

SEAN. Yeah a builder.

HAYLEY. So no building work today? Just chilling out?
Playing Monopoly. Taking it easy. Fooling around.

SEAN. Yeah.

HAYLEY. And dressing up in women's clothes?!

SEAN. Just Blake.

HAYLEY. The joker.

SEAN *looks back to the sitting room.*

Didn't know you were bald by the way. You always wear
that cute hat all the time. Looks like you shave it too. Is it a
fashion statement or something 'cause I quite like bald men.
Trying to impress me?

*She laughs a little. She's flirting with him.*

Sorry I'm talking so much. My mum reckons it's from
working at Tesco. You talk all day to the customers, get
home and I can't stop talking. It's not intentional! You get
stuck in a pattern. Christ, you've no idea what I mean, do
you?

SEAN. No I know what you mean.

HAYLEY. So was he serious? Your dad. He really wants me to
fix his lunch the way he said?

SEAN. He does, yeah.

HAYLEY. A bit rich though isn't it? I'm on my lunch break, I come up here as a favour and end up fixing his lunch.

SEAN. You've been very nice.

HAYLEY. Well, that's the Tesco training. It's all about customer care.

SEAN. Thank you.

HAYLEY. Thank you and have a nice day!

SEAN (*confused*). Okay.

HAYLEY. S'pose if I might get something out of it though?

*She takes a can of Harp out of the Tesco bag and smiles.*

A bit early but… after them stairs and…

*She opens the can of beer.*

DINNY *fires a look over at the kitchen as he hears the can open.*

HAYLEY *drinks some beer.*

BLAKE *does a perfect impersonation of* HAYLEY.

BLAKE. Looks like you shave it too. Are you trying to impress me?

HAYLEY *quickly turns and sees* BLAKE *looking in at her. She's a little nervous of him.*

HAYLEY. Very good. (*As* SEAN *takes her to one side.*) Why's he looking at me like that?

SEAN. Be honest with me please. Why did you come here?

*A pause.*

HAYLEY. To be nice. To do a nice thing.

*A pause.*

SEAN (*anxious*). But for no other reason, Hayley? Something you won't tell me?

HAYLEY. How d'you mean?

SEAN. Not to trick me?

*HAYLEY's a little confused. She just laughs.*

HAYLEY. Seriously?

*DINNY puts on the tape recorder and 'An Irish Lullaby' begins to play.*

*SEAN tenses up. It can only mean one thing.*

(*Of the music.*) That sounds nice. Quite old fashioned but I quite like that. (*Slight pause. Closes her eyes.*) Green grass. Stone walls. A little thatched cottage by the river. Little girl with red hair in ringlets sat on a donkey. (*Opening her eyes.*) Does it remind you of back home in Ireland?

SEAN. No.

*A pause. She can see that SEAN looks frightened of something.*

HAYLEY. I'm not here to trick you, Sean, honest.

*She tugs at his sleeve playfully.*

All right?

*Seeing this, BLAKE enters fast and takes SEAN by the hand in an act of possession.*

HAYLEY *backs away from them.*

Well, I suppose I'll get his lunch on then.

*The music continues.*

HAYLEY *prepares the lunch.*

DINNY *stands up and puts his wig back on and grooms himself in preparation.*

BLAKE *gathers up the Monopoly money, refills and resets the pillow into the coffin.*

SEAN *looks terrified.*

*Suddenly DINNY slams the tape recorder off.*

BLAKE *and* SEAN *race into the sitting room.*

*The Farce resumes with pace.* BLAKE *and* SEAN *are playing their younger selves.*

BLAKE. He's away like a bat of hell with the pole still dangling out his rear end and here we are with Finbarr's bloody arm needing some serious attention, Dad.

SEAN (*lowering his voice so* HAYLEY *doesn't hear*). Well all this talk of being out in the wild and surviving on the basics and what we did next just seemed the most natural.

BLAKE. Looking at his broken arm we decided to give it the snake bite treatment.

SEAN. So we pissed on him.

DINNY. Fair play.

BLAKE *grabs* SEAN *and quickly enters the kitchen with him.*

HAYLEY *turns to them.*

HAYLEY. D'you have any salt?

BLAKE AS JACK (*furious*). For Christ's sake, Peter. We shouldn't have bothered murdering this old shit.

*He takes a can of beer from* SEAN*'s hand.*

SEAN AS PETER. Keep your voice down, Jack.

BLAKE AS JACK (*draining the can of beer*). For all his money your father's worthless to us. This coffin is worth more than him.

BLAKE *pulls up the pillow.*

This ridiculous plump lining.

BLAKE *starts banging the pillow off the coffin.*

HAYLEY. Sean?

BLAKE AS JACK. Jesus the extravagance of the man. This silk bloody pillow with his initials on it for GOD'S SAKE!! I MEAN…

*The pillow rips.*

SEAN, BLAKE *and* HAYLEY *freeze as the Monopoly money falls around them.*

HAYLEY (*smiling*). Is this some sort of joke?

BLAKE *pulls* SEAN'*s arm and drags him back into the sitting room.*

DINNY. All right, boys, back in the back garden and behave yourself.

SEAN *and* BLAKE *disappear into the right wardrobe and reappear fast as* PADDY *and* EILEEN.

SEAN AS PADDY. Christ, Dinny, they're a handful, them kids. They wouldn't be my idea of children now.

HAYLEY *stands at the kitchen entrance. She's beginning to laugh at what's happening.*

DINNY. They wouldn't?

SEAN AS PADDY. I'd be of the thinking that children should be seen and not heard. Unless of course it was a children's choral choir in which case seeing and hearing would be an absolute delight.

HAYLEY *laughs a little.*

DINNY. Not at all, Paddy. Sure look at us. Raucous were we not? More than a handful. Two handfuls.

BLAKE AS EILEEN (*dreamily*). Bit of fighter were you, Denis?

DINNY. I was, Eileen. Back in the days when Cork City was dog rough, where to take a night-time stroll was an act of madness comparable to forcing long deadly skewers into your eyeballs, Cork was a jungle back then. And I'm not saying that I was its Tarzan…

SEAN AS PADDY. Because you can't swim.

DINNY. That's right, you're right. But I was more in the mode of King Kong, if you get my meaning. A gigantic freakish gorilla, intent on protecting his own and causing untold damage and chaos to those who challenge my jungle authority.

SEAN *looks towards* HAYLEY.

HAYLEY (*smiling*). It's good.

BLAKE AS EILEEN *gets closer to* DINNY.

BLAKE AS EILEEN (*whispering*). If only Jack had the same primal strength, the same domination.

DINNY (*whispering*). I know in this hour of grief I must be a symbol of reliability and power to you, Eileen. But I must warn you… flattery will get you into everywhere.

DINNY *and* BLAKE AS EILEEN *share a flirtatious laugh.*

BLAKE *and* SEAN *enter the kitchen fast, making* HAYLEY *step back into it.*

BLAKE AS JACK (*picking up the money*). How much do you think is here, Peter?

SEAN AS PETER. All of it maybe. These are big notes, Jack.

BLAKE AS JACK. Get it back in the coffin quick.

*They gather up the money and shove it in the coffin.*

HAYLEY. Can you stop just for a sec…

SEAN AS PETER. So what's our plan, Jack?

BLAKE AS JACK. Plan, plan, plan?! He stays here tonight. Tomorrow, me and you get him back in the hearse and drive. We pull over in a lay-by, divide the cash and get on with our new lives. Feck it, the sooner I leave that Eileen bitch and start to express myself the better!

SEAN AS PETER. Ah now that's my sister you're talking about, Jack.

BLAKE AS JACK. Oh the family man, are ya?! Filling your daddy with two bottles of gin, a bag of glue and strapping him into that speedboat, remember!

BLAKE AS JACK *grabs his beer and knocks it back*.

SEAN AS PETER (*peeved*). Why do you keep on taking my drink like that!?

DINNY (*explaining to* HAYLEY). Greedy Jack always hungry for the drink! Snatching it away at the last moment. Good detail, lads! We'll explain that in the finish! (*Prompting*.) Again, Blake, again!

BLAKE AS JACK. Filling your daddy with two bottles of gin, a bag of glue and strapping him into that speedboat, remember!

BLAKE AS JACK *grabs his beer and knocks it back*.

SEAN AS PETER (*peeved*). Why do you keep on taking my drink like that!?

DINNY. Excellent, boys!

BLAKE AS MAUREEN. Is everyone going to have chicken?

SEAN AS PETER *and* BLAKE AS JACK (*a scream*). Ahhh!

HAYLEY (*annoyed*). Helloooooooo!

BLAKE AS JACK (*whispering*). Who the hell's that?

SEAN AS PETER (*whispering*). The painter's wife, Maureen.

BLAKE AS JACK. Shit. Shit! (*Addressing* MAUREEN.) How much of that did you hear, Maureen?

BLAKE AS MAUREEN. Hearse. Lay-by. Dividing the cash.

BLAKE AS JACK. Well, it is ours.

BLAKE AS MAUREEN. What about Mrs Cotter?

SEAN AS PETER. Her husband Jack here's looking after her share.

HAYLEY. Right, I'm off then, Sean!

BLAKE AS JACK. It's not like it's any of your business anyway, Maureen.

HAYLEY. Sean!

SEAN AS PETER. It'll be our little secret then, Maureen?

BLAKE AS MAUREEN. I'll get on with the food so.

*Irritated,* HAYLEY *grabs her coat and bag and leaves the kitchen and heads for the front door.*

DINNY *looks at her as she tries to open the locks on the door.*

HAYLEY (*exasperated*). Oh open the fucking door!

DINNY *suddenly pounces on her and grabs her by the throat, pinning her to the door. He takes her bag and throws it to one side.*

SEAN *and* BLAKE *come out from the kitchen and stand by, watching.*

DINNY. Don't scream now.

HAYLEY, *terrified, looks towards* SEAN.

Here to break us up, boys. Trick us and drag us down to the street.

HAYLEY (*quietly*). What?

DINNY. Just do what I asked and you won't be hurt.

HAYLEY*'s eyes fill with tears.*

HAYLEY. But what are you doing?

*A pause.*

Why are you all doing this?

*A pause as* DINNY *just looks at her.*

DINNY. You be a good girl, take off your coat and do what I asked ya.

BLAKE *helps her off with her coat and immediately puts it on. Again he perfectly impersonates her.*

BLAKE. Thank you and have a nice day!

HAYLEY (*to* SEAN). Do something, Sean!

DINNY *turns* SEAN *towards him*.

DINNY. 'Feck it, Dinny, I don't…'

SEAN. Dad, please…

DINNY. 'Feck it, Dinny…'

SEAN. We can't keep her like this!

BLAKE. SAY IT, SEAN! SAY IT!

BLAKE *and* DINNY *side by side wait for* SEAN *to get back on track*.

SEAN *looks back at* HAYLEY.

HAYLEY. Please.

*Then, slowly:*

SEAN AS PADDY. Feck it, Dinny, I don't like that Peter fella at all! Closer he's getting to my Vera and the way he's looking down at me…

DINNY. Easy, Paddy. It's a walk in the garden you need.

HAYLEY *walks back into the kitchen as the three just look at her.*

Again, Sean! Come on! Come on!

SEAN AS PADDY (*more energy*). Feck it, Dinny, I don't like that Peter fella at all! Closer he's getting to my Vera and the way he's looking down at me…

DINNY. Easy, Paddy. It's a walk in the garden you need.

SEAN AS PADDY. I understand the stress you brain surgeons are under but I don't see you patronising me like that.

DINNY. Good man, Sean!

SEAN AS PADDY. You're not embarrassed of me are you?

DINNY. What?

BLAKE *takes off* HAYLEY'*s coat and drops it on the floor. He stands at the kitchen entrance looking in at her.*

SEAN AS PADDY. Embarrassed of me. Tell me straight, are ya, Dinny?

DINNY. Embarrassed of you? Embarrassed of my own little brother? A man who lives in abject poverty in a hovel in London. A brother so ugly that when he was born, the doctors thought our mother had pushed out her perforated poisoned liver. A man who as a boy was so unpopular that even his imaginary friends would beat him up. A brother so stupid that for twenty years he thought that Irish dancing was a running event for people who were afraid to travel.

SEAN AS PADDY. You're not embarrassed of me then?

DINNY *gives him a look.*

DINNY. Keep an eye on Blake and Sean for us, Paddy, and make sure they don't torture anything.

SEAN AS PADDY. Righty ho!

SEAN *enters the right wardrobe. From inside an enormous scream of anguish:*

SEAN. FUCK!

BLAKE *and* DINNY *look towards the wardrobe and* DINNY *starts to laugh.*

DINNY. Good, Blake.

BLAKE. Thanks, Dad.

DINNY. Off ya go, son.

BLAKE *quickly puts on* EILEEN*'s wig and walks into the bedroom and sees the coffin.*

BLAKE AS EILEEN. Oh my God what's this?!

SEAN *arrives fast as* PETER*, and, seeing the coffin:*

SEAN AS PETER. What the hell?!

BLAKE AS EILEEN. Who is that?

SEAN AS PETER. What's that smell of whiskey?

DINNY. It's my mother.

BLAKE AS EILEEN. What's your mother doing on my dining-room table, Denis?

DINNY. She's dead.

BLAKE AS EILEEN. You bring your dead mother on jobs with you?

SEAN AS PETER. You're using my sister's house for your dead mother's wake! You sneak!

BLAKE AS EILEEN. Oh, Denis...

DINNY (*snaps*). It's for Paddy! I know I shouldn't be here but I was doing it all for Paddy... because of his... condition.

BLAKE AS EILEEN. What condition, Denis?

*A pause.*

DINNY. Paddy's fallen on rough times, Eileen. Him and his wife Vera live destitute in a towerblock in London.

BLAKE AS EILEEN. So?

DINNY (*obviously thinking on his feet*). One day last year... Paddy, cold and shivering... walked down the Walworth Road and into a pet shop for some warmth. He was in there looking at the guppies in their tanks and talking to the budgies in their cages. The owner figured out that he was a retard so he let him at it.

BLAKE AS EILEEN (*lost*). Okay.

DINNY. Now Paddy was ravenous with the hunger. The last bit of solid to pass his lips was the nib of a bookie's pen and that was a whole week ago. There in the back of the pet shop, slunked in the corner... in an old crate... was a giant snake... called... the... (*Thinks hard.*) Big... Langer Snake... eating a carrot. Well, Paddy, God bless him, didn't give it much thought, reached in and grabbed that Langer's dinner. When SNAP! Paddy was bitten and infected with a terrible snake venom.

BLAKE AS EILEEN. So is he dying?

DINNY. He will die, yeah. In the meantime his infected brain has started an unrelenting rot.

SEAN AS PETER. That would explain all his brain-surgeon nonsense.

DINNY. I took him here as a special treat, honest, Eileen. We were meant to bury Mammy today but Paddy wouldn't part with her. You arrived with your terrible news about your dead daddy and for some reason… Paddy's convinced that you're all brain surgeons intent on removing that snake venom from his miniscule brain.

*Slight pause.*

BLAKE AS EILEEN. I might have known that your reasons were for reasons of love. It's a wonderful thing to see such a bond between two family members.

SEAN AS PETER (*with true regret*). It's not always the case with us, is it, Eileen?

BLAKE AS EILEEN. With Denis's inspiration… I'm sure we can change, little brother.

*A slight pause.*

DINNY (*with relief and immense self-satisfaction*). Well, I don't know about you two but I could murder a drink!

DINNY *pops open a well-earned can of Harp.*

BLAKE AS JACK. I've been in the kitchen counting all the money. We're looking at fifty grand each, Peter!

SEAN AS PETER. I'm starting to feel uneasy about this.

BLAKE AS JACK. Uneasy?! Uneasy?! What do you mean?

SEAN AS PETER. Orchestrating Daddy's death was one thing but I can't stab my own sister in the back. It's her money too, Jack.

BLAKE AS JACK (*grabbing* SEAN AS PETER). Listen to me, you little shit! We had a deal. You've seen how she's treated me. Bullied in my own home so I have to spend my days sneaking around in the garden shed and drinking methylated spirits to keep myself sane!

SEAN AS PETER. Yes I…

BLAKE AS JACK. I deserve that money, you said so yourself. You back out on me now and I'll make shit of you, do you hear me! I'll have you, Peter. You and your sister, I swear it, man!

SEAN AS PETER. Oh Jack, come on!

*BLAKE AS JACK suddenly smacks SEAN AS PETER hard across the face. A little too hard.*

*SEAN, taken aback, dives at BLAKE. The two fall to the ground and start to fight each other.*

*DINNY nonchalantly walks past them and over to the kitchen and HAYLEY.*

*He looks at her for some time.*

DINNY. How's my chicken coming along?

*A slight pause.*

HAYLEY. It's heating in the oven.

DINNY. A lovely smell… roasting chicken.

*HAYLEY remains quiet.*

*DINNY drinks from his can of Harp.*

Thirsty work this. Drama piling on, isn't it?

HAYLEY. Yeah.

DINNY. Impressive work. Wonderful detail. (*A pause.*) Who d'you reckon has the best chance with the acting trophy today? Me is it? I'd be the best one, would I? Don't be shy!

HAYLEY. I suppose.

*A pause.*

DINNY. You're black. What are we going to do about that, Maureen?

*DINNY continues to drink his can of Harp and look at her.*

*BLAKE has SEAN on the ground and is strangling him.*

*Realising what he's doing, BLAKE stops. He remains sitting on SEAN's chest looking down on him.*

BLAKE (*quietly*). Were you talking to her about us? Are you trying to find ways to get us down to the streets? Send the little girl up and the door starts banging with more bodies wanting to get us. Are you turning your back on me, Sean?

DINNY *stands at the kitchen entrance looking in on the two of them.*

SEAN. I wouldn't do that. I couldn't be alone outside without you, Blake.

BLAKE. But you're wanting me to kill Dad, aren't you, Sean? We kill Dad, break the story, step outside like you've got it all planned… but then you walk away from me with her.

SEAN. With her?

BLAKE. You love her, tell me.

SEAN. Blake, we can both leave here. Me and you.

BLAKE. You can't deny you love her!

SEAN. You don't have to be scared of what's out there any more.

BLAKE. WE BELONG IN HERE!

SEAN. Blake…

BLAKE *slaps him hard across the face.*

*He climbs off* SEAN *and stands over him.*

BLAKE. You break what I know and I give you my word, little brother, I'll have to kill you. (*Less sure.*) I can kill you straight.

SEAN. Then you'll live with what he lives with…

BLAKE. It's not true.

SEAN. I saw him, Blake. I saw the blood that day! It's all lies!

BLAKE. It was Mr Cotter and the poisoned chicken…

SEAN. Jesus, Blake…

BLAKE. No, Sean, no! No no no no!

SEAN. Blake!

BLAKE *covers his ears and enters the bedroom and lies on the bed with his head beneath the pillow.*

SEAN *remains lying on the floor. He then notices* DINNY *standing looking down at him. He must have heard what he just said.*

DINNY. All a little bit fucked today, isn't it, Sean?

SEAN. Yes, Dad.

DINNY. Come here to me so.

DINNY *walks back inside the kitchen.*

SEAN *gets up and walks inside too.*

HAYLEY *stands at the cooker and* DINNY *sits at the table.* SEAN *stands by the entrance.*

*A pause.*

Tell me what you remember the day I left Cork, Sean.

SEAN. Why?

DINNY. Well, is it the same as the way we tell it?

*A pause.*

SEAN. No.

*A pause.*

DINNY. No? (*He's angry but keeps calm. A pause.*) Let me hear it so I can see where I stand with ya. You're playing in Mrs Cotter's back garden.

SEAN (*a pause*). No, Dad. We're playing in our back garden me and Blake. Granny's coffin's open in the front room and the room smells of dust so you send us out into the fresh air. We're lying on the grass and we're talking about what we'll be when we're all grown up. Blake full of talk about being an astronaut. He's read a book on it and he knows some big words to do with space. He says he'd feel safe up there. He said if he got nervous he'd hide the Earth behind his thumb.

He talked about a parade in Dublin when the space men got back from space. How there'd have to be a special parade for him in Cork and everyone would come out and cheer him on and slag off the Dubs. We're just sitting on the grass chatting like that. (*A pause.*) I say I want to be a bus driver because I like buses and Blake thinks that it's a great job. Just like driving a rocket 'cept your orbit's the Grand Parade and Mac Curtain Street. (*A pause.*) There's shouting from inside the house. You and Uncle Paddy screaming at each other. Fighting over Granny's money even before she's stuck in the ground. Aunty Vera crying her cries real high like a baby crying. Your voice so much bigger than Uncle Paddy and him saying, 'No, Dinny, no please, Dinny!' (*Slight pause.*) And then we hear Mammy screaming, Dad. We're both up fast and running through our back door and into our kitchen and the smell of the roast chicken. Her screaming coming from the sitting room and Blake won't go inside 'cause he's frightened of what he might see. But I do. I do go inside. And Mammy grabs me and spins me around fast so I can't see… but I see Uncle Paddy and Aunty Vera on the ground and I see you standing in the corner with blood all over your hands. There's blood on your hands and a kitchen knife, I'm sure of it. (*A pause.*) Mam's terrible screaming. And you're standing at the door and I can see that you're trying to make up your mind whether to stay or to run. And Mammy kisses you and says, 'Leave, now', and sets you free. You just step out to the outside and begin your run.

*A long pause.*

DINNY. Why did your mammy send you two little boys right after me if I did a bad thing?

SEAN. Because she still loved you. Because what we had used to be so good in Ireland. Maybe she could forgive you. (*Slight pause.*) Dad, I don't know why she sent us.

*A pause.*

*Momentarily,* DINNY *is affected by what* SEAN *says.*

DINNY. I'm keeping you and Blake safe.

SEAN. I know you think that.

DINNY (*aggravated now*). FUCK!!

> HAYLEY *flinches*.
>
> (*Quickly*.) So what did you two talk about?
>
> DINNY *turns* HAYLEY *around to face him*.
>
> You talked this morning in Tesco, didn't you? Talkin' about what we get up to in here, Sean?

SEAN. No, Dad.

> DINNY *places* SEAN *opposite* HAYLEY.

DINNY. Don't be lying to me and tell me what was said. Show me exactly how it was. The same words. Play it. (*To* HAYLEY.) Sit down!

> *He sits* HAYLEY *down by the table*.
>
> (*To* SEAN.) You walk up to her and you say:

HAYLEY. All right?

DINNY. And you say what then?

SEAN. Hello.

DINNY. Do the shopping, come on, come on!

> HAYLEY *mimes scanning* SEAN*'s shopping*.
>
> DINNY *mimes packing the shopping into a plastic bag*.
>
> (*To* HAYLEY.) And you say?

HAYLEY. Same shopping as usual? (*Breaks*.) Look, please let me leave!

DINNY (*snaps*). Again again!

HAYLEY. Same shopping as usual?

SEAN. And I laugh a little for no good reason. (*Slight pause. To* HAYLEY.) I'm so sorry.

> HAYLEY *breaks down again*.

DINNY *shakes her to talk. A pause as she controls herself.*

HAYLEY. Are you doing anything at the weekend? It's just I might go down to Brighton Beach, have you ever been there?

SEAN. No.

HAYLEY. It's nice. Maybe you'd like to go there with me sometime.

BLAKE *appears out of the bedroom and stands listening to* SEAN *and* HAYLEY *talking in the kitchen.*

SEAN. And I can't say anything as I pack the shopping away. (*Slight pause.*) But I'm thinking of whether I could ever risk my life with somebody else. If there would ever come a time when someone would promise me a new start. I'm thinking about us walking on a beach by the sea and I'm wondering if you'd stay with me if I got outside, Hayley. But you can't see me thinking about all of that. And I want to say, 'I'd really like to go there one day.'

HAYLEY *almost smiles.*

HAYLEY. Then I would say, 'Let's go, Sean. Let's leave now.'

*A slight pause.*

SEAN (*quietly*). You would?

BLAKE *hits the play button on the tape recorder and 'A Nation Once Again' blares loudly out.*

*He starts to thrash the flat.*

DINNY *goes to the sitting room to see him. He starts to laugh.*

DINNY. Good man, Blake! That a boy! Go on now! Go on, Blake!

*Everything's unravelling.*

SEAN *looks very worried. Suddenly he notices* HAYLEY*'s holding his hand.*

*She gestures that her phone is in her bag in the sitting room and that* SEAN *should get it.*

DINNY *turns and grabs* SEAN *and throws him out into the sitting room.*

BLAKE *continues demolishing the flat as* SEAN *watches him.*

DINNY *turns off the music.*

(*Snaps.*) Enough, Blake!

BLAKE *stops. He stares at* SEAN, *strikes him hard across the face.*

SEAN *hits the ground.*

BLAKE AS JACK (*announcing*). Anyone care where I am… I'm in the garden shed!

BLAKE AS JACK *walks quickly away and enters a wardrobe and closes the door.*

DINNY (*threatening* SEAN). You back down, do you hear me?

BLAKE *re-enters fast as* VERA *and heads for* SEAN AS PETER *as he gets up.*

BLAKE AS VERA. Did Jack hurt you, Peter love? You had an argument, did ya?! I know what you science types are like. Fierce competitive. Good Christ, I like your style! You make my Paddy look like another species.

SEAN AS PETER (*dazed*). I can't understand what you're doing with Paddy, Vera. Having loyalty to a man with his condition.

BLAKE AS VERA. Sure Paddy's hole is only a part of his problem.

SEAN AS PETER. What a beautiful lady you are.

BLAKE AS VERA. At last someone to scoop me up in their arms and ride me horse back down Walworth Road to sunnier and better climes!

SEAN *returns to the wardrobe.*

DINNY (*walking into the bedroom, mid-conversation*). I hear what you're saying, Eileen, but I've only got so much love to spread about, darling.

BLAKE AS EILEEN. But that wife of yours!

DINNY. Boring she might be. The personality of a dead fish, she most certainly has, but what Maureen can do in the kitchen. Like a wizard in there.

BLAKE AS EILEEN. But in the bedroom, Denis? How is she in the bedroom.

DINNY. She can give as good as she gets.

BLAKE AS EILEEN. You see that's the sort of talk I like to hear from a real man!

DINNY. Oh now, Eileen, please! There's one thing cheating on my unsuspecting and stupid wife and another thing entirely bringing disgrace on my dear mother as she lies in her eternal sleep.

SEAN *opens the wardrobe door to sneak out into the room and get* HAYLEY*'s bag.*

BLAKE AS EILEEN. Such a strange expression she has on her face, Denis.

BLAKE AS EILEEN *looks in the coffin,*

DINNY. She has. As if she's bitten into a lemon.

BLAKE AS EILEEN. Not the sort of face you want to wear in eternal life.

DINNY. That's true… but the poor love didn't have a choice. Reconstructed her head and face was… Hang on a sec…

SEAN *is back in the wardrobe fast as* DINNY *walks from the bedroom through the sitting room and into the kitchen.*

(*Glancing at* HAYLEY.) Carry on, carry on!

*He takes up a washing-up-liquid bottle and fills it with water.*

*He returns to the bedroom with the bottle and takes up his position.*

Again, Blake.

BLAKE AS EILEEN. Such a strange expression she has on her face, Denis.

DINNY. She has. As if she's bitten into a lemon, Eileen.

BLAKE AS EILEEN. Not the sort of face you want to wear in eternal life.

DINNY. That's true… but the poor love didn't have a choice. Reconstructed her head and face was but…

*He squirts some water from the bottle into his eyes to effect tears.*

(*Getting emotional.*) …but not by the highly qualified surgeon as we wished, Eileen. It was a price we couldn't afford.

BLAKE AS EILEEN. Whose hands done the deed so, Denis?

DINNY. The hands and the deed were mine, Eileen. Though to be honest I can't remember much about it. It wouldn't be every day that a son is called upon to stitch up his dead mother's pulverised face, so I had a few drinks to lessen the shock. The only previous stitching experience I had was a scarf I knitted when I was a schoolboy.

BLAKE AS EILEEN. Is that what accounts for the length of her chin?

DINNY. It is.

BLAKE AS EILEEN. And the little bobbles at the end?

DINNY. I was getting carried away at that point.

DINNY *looks at the bottle.*

Genius! Fucking genius, boy!

DINNY *runs from the bedroom and into the sitting room. He grabs the acting trophy from its shelf and kisses it.*

Is there anyone better?! Might I ever be challenged, tell me!?

SEAN AS PADDY *appears, thundering out of the wardrobe. His performance seemingly back on track.*

SEAN AS PADDY. It's Mrs Cotter's house!?! Say it isn't so, Dinny. Say it isn't so! Lying to me like that. You of the red wine and green Pringles!

DINNY. Ah bollix!

SEAN AS PADDY. That Mr Cotter told me whose house it is before he legged it into that garden shed. You know of the poverty…

DINNY. '… before he legged it into that garden shed and into that yellow frock.' Fuck it, Sean, come on, COME ON, BOY! Mr Cotter, yellow frock, poison in the bucket, making the blue sauce for the cooked chicken! Details, details!

SEAN. I remember, Dad!

DINNY. Remember nothing! Say the line!

SEAN AS PADDY. That Mr Cotter told me whose house it is before he legged it into that garden shed and into that yellow frock! You know of the terrible poverty me and Vera are under. You whisk us up here with your airs and graces, spin out Mammy's will and fob me off with a monthly allowance and three cans of Harp. Shame on you! Shame on you, Dinny!

*When* DINNY *turns away,* SEAN *grabs* HAYLEY*'s bag from off the floor and hides it behind his back.*

DINNY. He's losing it big time, Eileen.

SEAN AS PADDY. Losing nothing. Gaining is what I'm doing. Gaining my rightful half to Mammy's estate.

BLAKE AS VERA. You using a time of grief to rob a man of his rightful inheritance!

SEAN AS PADDY. Go on, Vera! Go on!!

BLAKE AS VERA. Any man with average intelligence would have copped onto you a long time ago, Dinny. But you taking advantage of Paddy's tiny minuscule brain. A man who thought that cats laid eggs. That Walt Disney discovered America...

SEAN AS PADDY. All right, Vera...

BLAKE AS VERA.... and that fish actually had fingers. Well, shame on you for this, Dinny!

DINNY (*snaps*). Yerrah, shut up out of that with your 'shame'!

DINNY *crashes into the kitchen as does* BLAKE, *who's now playing* MAUREEN.

HAYLEY*'s startled.*

Fuck it, Maureen we're fucked!

BLAKE AS MAUREEN. What, love?

DINNY. Paddy and Vera knows whose house it is, pet. Time to pack up Mammy and get the hell out of here.

BLAKE AS MAUREEN. Smashed are we?

DINNY. Dead in the water, love. Might get a few bob for Mammy's coffin, otherwise we're smashed.

BLAKE AS MAUREEN. Take a look in there and see if it doesn't cheer you up.

DINNY *looks and holds up some Monopoly money.*

DINNY. Holy be jaynee! What's this!?

BLAKE AS MAUREEN. Only them two other men know of it. It's half Mrs Cotter's but she doesn't have a clue, Dinny. If there was any way we could swindle the money out of her.

DINNY. Swindle this money out of Mrs Cotter, but how??!

DINNY *and* BLAKE *walk fast out of the kitchen and through the sitting room.*

A word in your ear, Eileen.

SEAN *throws the bag in to* HAYLEY.

BLAKE AS EILEEN. Why's it you told your brother Paddy that this was your house, Denis?

*In her hand,* HAYLEY*'s mobile phone suddenly plays the Crazy Frog version of Destiny Child's 'I'm a Survivor'.*

HAYLEY. Shit shit!

DINNY. What the fuck is that?!

SEAN *grabs* EILEEN*'s wig off* BLAKE *and continues speaking so as to mask the phone noise.*

SEAN AS EILEEN. Why's it you told your brother Paddy this was your house, Denis?

DINNY (*distracted*). 'Cause it's a deep bond between me and you, Eileen. For bonded through grief and tragedy we are.

DINNY *looking for the source of the noise.*

SEAN AS EILEEN. Tragedy, Denis? *Cein fath?*

BLAKE *is confused as he takes the wig back from* SEAN.

DINNY. That horse which killed your dear daddy as he sped through that field in his speedboat… that very same horse crushed my mammy as she picked gooseberries on a quiet country road.

*The ring tone stops.*

BLAKE AS EILEEN. The very same horse that my Dad ploughed into?

DINNY. That's the one.

BLAKE AS EILEEN. She was killed by my father so?

DINNY. And here we are left picking up the pieces, Eileen.

SEAN AS EILEEN. For her to be slain by my own father. If there was any way I could financially compensate you for this great tragedy. Anything… Anything at all…

BLAKE *suddenly realises something is up.*

HAYLEY *hides beneath the kitchen table.*

HAYLEY (*talking into the phone*). Mum, it's me! I'm in a flat on the Walworth Road… Will you stop talking and listen to me!

*BLAKE grabs HAYLEY from beneath the table. She screams and drops the phone.*

*DINNY is furious that the Farce has broken down once again.*

DINNY (*shouts*). Ah for fuck's sake!

*BLAKE drags HAYLEY screaming across the sitting room, picks up her coat and gets her inside the bedroom.*

*DINNY holds SEAN back as he tries to stop BLAKE. He fires him against the wardrobe.*

*SEAN collapses on the ground.*

*DINNY enters the kitchen and sees the phone on the ground.*

*BLAKE has thrown HAYLEY on the bed and is tying her arms behind her back. He then begins to gag her to stop her screaming.*

*DINNY picks up the phone and is amazed by it. He listens to the frantic voice on the other end.*

Hello? Am I holding a phone?

*He opens the oven door and throws the phone inside and slams the door shut.*

*He takes the large kitchen knife from the table and leaves the kitchen. He grabs SEAN by the hair and drags him to the armchair, making him sit.*

*Standing behind him he holds the knife hard against SEAN's throat.*

*BLAKE steps back from HAYLEY who lies face down on the bed, her arms bound. He then puts on her coat.*

SEAN. I won't go on.

DINNY. Of course you will.

SEAN. I can't, Dad.

DINNY. Sean…

SEAN. Dad, please, I can't do it any more.

DINNY *presses the knife in harder into* SEAN*'s throat.*

BLAKE *goes to the bedroom door and looks into the sitting room at the two of them.*

DINNY. Mammy making the macaroni cheese on a Tuesday, Sean. The two washed boys wrapped up in their dressing gowns on Saturday nights. Sunday morning and the four of us watching the Walton family on the telly with our dinner cooking in the kitchen. Friday night and in the pub for a feed of pints but I'm back home to kiss you little boys to beddy-byes just like Daddy Walton would. (*Slight pause.*) The family routine keeping things safe, Sean. I lived like that in Cork. I was a good man. (*A long pause.*) You looking in at Paddy and Vera dead on the floor like you said. My hand shaking. Real blood on the carpet. Me telling your mam, 'I'm off to London to make my fortune, Maureen. I'll send for you, Maureen, and we will be happy.' Her little kiss to me and telling me, 'Leave now.' I'm about to leave but I see you looking at me. Looking for answers, aren't ya? I turn and go. I go. In London and I'm standing in the roundabout in Elephant and Castle with all its noise and people, fuck it. 'Run, Dinny boy. Run.' Start running and get inside to Paddy's flat. These pictures of Paddy and Vera on the walls looking down at me, you see them? Asking me questions I can't answer, Sean. With every breath more scared of them. (*Slight pause.*) There's a knock on the door and it's you two boys standing there off the bus from Cork City, by jaynee. Sent by Mammy to ask me back to Cork, aren't ya. My little boys back to me. 'Hello little boys. Come on in, boys.' I wrap you up in a towel and hold ya. 'All right boys! Sure it's Daddy here, look. Ohh my little John Boy and Jim Bob! It's lovely to see ya again, boys!' To calm you down, Sean, I start to tell you the story of me and Paddy on Robert's Cove beach. Me with Daddy's towel wrapping Paddy up and keeping him safe. For days I play that story over and over for you and Blakey and it brings us some calm and peace of mind. The telling of the story... it helps me, Sean. (*A pause.*) 'Daddy?' 'Yes, Seanie?' 'What happened back home in Cork, Daddy?' (*A pause.*) I start to tell a new story. (*Almost breaks.*) My head, Sean.

DINNY *clutches at his head in real pain.*

SEAN *just looks at him.*

*The pain slowly goes. He lowers his hands from his head.*

*A pause.*

DINNY *looks right through him.*

We're making a routine that keeps our family safe. Isn't that what we've done here?

*A slight pause.*

SEAN. But none of these words are true.

*A pause.*

DINNY. It's my truth, nothing else matters. (*A pause.*) You can never leave here without poor Blake, can you, Sean?

SEAN. No, Dad.

DINNY. 'No, Dad.' To step outside and just little you all alone out there in the world, imagine that?

SEAN*'s eyes fill with tears.*

It could never happen, Sean, answer me.

SEAN. I couldn't be alone outside, Dad.

DINNY. No need, Seanie boy, no need at all.

SEAN *crying a little and* DINNY *embraces him.*

*A pause.*

You'll never tell Blake what you seen that last day, Sean?

SEAN. I wouldn't do that to him.

DINNY. A simple boy best kept in the dark, isn't he?

SEAN. It's a better place to be.

*A pause.*

DINNY. To kill me would only turn you into your dad. Isn't that what you're thinking, Sean? Answer me, boy.

*A long pause.*

So you're not going to kill me then?

*A pause.*

Hah?

SEAN *doesn't answer.*

*Hearing enough,* BLAKE *returns to* HAYLEY *and starts to untie her.*

It would never happen on *The Waltons*. Can't imagine John Boy or Jim Bob raising a nasty hand to Daddy Walton, can ya? Never in a million years, despite all those wood-carving tools hanging about their house, would you see such a thing on Walton Mountain, Sean.

*The embrace breaks and* DINNY *looks at* SEAN.

Get back to my story. Get ready for the big finish, Sean. Soon Paddy's hole will strike and off to meet the good Lord, God bless him. Play it big and clear for me, won't ya?

SEAN. I will, Dad.

DINNY. Acting trophy could be yours, Sean. I'm rooting for you, boy.

*A pause.*

SEAN. Will you let her go when we finish today?

DINNY. I will let her go if you're a good boy to me.

SEAN. All right, Dad.

HAYLEY *sits on the bed with* BLAKE *standing in her coat looking down at her.*

HAYLEY. Do you want to be me?

BLAKE. No.

BLAKE *takes off her coat and hands it to her.*

HAYLEY. How long have you been doing this? (*Slight pause.*) Can't you leave?

BLAKE *doesn't answer. A pause.*

BLAKE. If Sean can go, you'll be with him? You won't leave Sean alone outside, promise me.

*A slight pause.*

HAYLEY. I'll stay with him.

BLAKE. Cross your heart and hope to die.

*A slight pause.*

HAYLEY. Cross my heart and hope to die.

*A pause.*

BLAKE. I can finish it so.

*For the final time* DINNY *plays 'A Nation Once Again' on the tape recorder.*

BLAKE *and* SEAN *take up their positions.* BLAKE *goes to the kitchen and stands looking into the coffin as* EILEEN *and* SEAN *stands where* SEAN AS PADDY *was standing previously.*

DINNY *looks at* HAYLEY *as she makes her way back over to the kitchen. She drops her coat by the door.*

*She looks towards* SEAN *and him at her. But she knows she's by herself now. She enters the kitchen and finishes preparing the lunch.*

*Everything in its proper place and* DINNY *turns off the tape recorder and enters the kitchen fast.*

DINNY. So what exactly are you saying about compensation, Eileen, for my mother's death at the hands of your daddy's speedboat. We can go halves, is it?

BLAKE AS EILEEN. This terrific money could all be yours, Denis. Just say the word and it could be you and me…

BLAKE AS MAUREEN (*snaps*). Dinny!

DINNY *and* BLAKE AS EILEEN (*startled*). Ahhh!

DINNY. Yerrah for fuck sake, Maureen, do you have to creep around like that!?

BLAKE AS MAUREEN. It's the money you're after and not that slapper, right? (*Pleading*.) You wouldn't leave me for Eileen, Dinny?

DINNY (*whispering*). Course I wouldn't, sweetheart. You'll have plenty of dinner days ahead of ya. Now shut up and cook!

DINNY *exits the kitchen.* SEAN AS PADDY *turns away from him and enters the bedroom.*

SEAN AS PADDY. There he is, the man who tried to rob me blind.

BLAKE *enters the stage right wardrobe.*

Stay away from me now for I have no family but for Mammy here.

DINNY. She's dead, Paddy. She's dead.

SEAN AS PADDY. I'm aware she's dead, Dinny. Well aware of that fact. You've tricked me for the last time, boy! A brother of mine you are no longer.

BLAKE *re-enters as* JACK *wearing a yellow frock. He holds a bucket with a yellow poison symbol painted on it. He enters the kitchen and starts to boil up some milk in a pan, and empties some of the blue contents of the bucket into it.* HAYLEY *looks on.*

DINNY. Seeing our dead mammy on that country road it threw me into a terrible despair. Lies I started to spin. Lies against the only brother I ever had. Sure I couldn't carry on with you cut out from my life, Paddy.

SEAN AS PADDY. You have done for ten years.

DINNY. That's right, you're right. But this afternoon has set me straight, Paddy. The bond is being built, I swear it.

SEAN AS PADDY. It is?

DINNY. You're my brother, Paddy, and for the life of me I don't know why I like ya. A sad day today with our mammy stuck in that box but a happy day for our reunion. So what say you of a reconciliation, oh little brother of mine? (*He holds out a can of beer.*)

SEAN AS PADDY *grabs it and knocks it back fast.*

SEAN *exits the bedroom and meets* BLAKE *who exits the kitchen where he's left* HAYLEY *stirring the pan of milk.*

BLAKE AS VERA. Mr Cotter's in the kitchen, Peter, with a bucket of poison! A yellow frock he has on! I caught Paddy wearing a pair of my knickers once. Standing on a chair and hanging a light bulb he was. It was like watching *The Dam Busters*. Sooner or later the walls of them knickers were bound to…

SEAN AS PETER. You know it's difficult for me to be hearing that, Vera sweetheart.

BLAKE AS VERA. You can imagine what it was like seeing it.

SEAN AS PETER. So Jack must be planning to poison me and my sister Eileen so the money can all be his. Well, we'll see about that!

BLAKE *enters the kitchen as* JACK.

BLAKE AS JACK. Just pour it over the chicken like I said, Maureen! I'm not standing here arguing with you about savoury sauces when there's a coffin of money that needs liberating.

*During the following,* SEAN *lights a fire lighter and throws it into the right wardrobe.*

DINNY (*entering kitchen*). Ah Mr Cotter!

BLAKE AS JACK. Suppose you're wondering what I'm doing wearing this yellow frock?

DINNY. Looks like you're making a sauce for the chicken, Jack.

BLAKE AS JACK. True but the bigger picture will speak of my new-found freedom, Denis.

DINNY. A fight worth fighting for if you don't mind me saying so, Jackie.

*DINNY pats him on the backside.*

BLAKE AS JACK. Exactly the sort of confidence boost that's needed before facing the dragon-lady herself!

*BLAKE exits the kitchen.*

Afternoon, Eileen!

BLAKE AS EILEEN (*screeches*). Oh my sweet Jesus!

*Suddenly BLAKE covers SEAN's mouth with his hand.*

BLAKE. I'm ready to kill her if that's what it takes.

*SEAN, freaked, slaps his hand away.*

SEAN. No, Blake!

BLAKE. Just like Dad, Sean!

DINNY (*to* HAYLEY). What the hell's he up to, Maureen?

*Slight pause.*

HAYLEY. What?

*BLAKE and SEAN freeze and look through the open kitchen door.*

DINNY (*smiling*). So you got the lunch made the way I told ya, Maureen?

HAYLEY. Yeah.

DINNY. 'Yes, Dinny.'

HAYLEY. Yes, Dinny.

DINNY. Good girl. Little pink wafers too?

HAYLEY. I broke them up and made them into a heart shape like you said.

*He smiles back to BLAKE and SEAN.*

DINNY. Good work, Maureen. And what's that weird smell, love?

HAYLEY. Just coloured milk, I think.

DINNY *takes* MAUREEN*'s wig off* BLAKE*'s head and puts it on* HAYLEY.

BLAKE *gets the kitchen knife from the coffee table.* SEAN *tries to wrestle it off him.*

DINNY. What's that weird smell, love? (*Instructing* HAYLEY *in her line.*) 'You've got to stay away from the chicken, Dinny.'

HAYLEY (*crying, slowly*). You've got to stay away from the chicken, Dinny.

DINNY. Oh Jesus, love, I can't. Sure amn't I famished for chicken. A day of deceit and lies and I'm fit to eat a horse, by jaynee. (*Instructing her.*) 'Mr Cotter's trying to poison his wife and Peter with the chicken.'

BLAKE *walks fast into the wardrobe.*

SEAN *relieved that he's gone but still freaked out.*

HAYLEY. Mr Cotter's trying to poison his wife and Peter with the chicken.

DINNY. Poison, Maureen?

HAYLEY (*offering a new line*). Well, I saw Mr Cotter with a bucket of poison. He got me to mix it with the milk to pour it over the chicken.

DINNY (*impressed*). So he wants you to put the poisoned sauce on the chicken to kill Peter and Eileen and trick them by saying that it is in fact your special sauce, Maureen?

HAYLEY. I suppose.

DINNY (*explaining*). See, that way Peter and Vera will take the poisoned chicken thinking that it's just one of Maureen's savoury sensations. Do your new line again.

HAYLEY. I saw Mr Cotter with a bucket of poison. He got me to mix it with the milk to pour it over the chicken.

DINNY. Well, far be it for me to stand in his way. Pour away, Maureen!

DINNY *makes* HAYLEY *pour the sky-blue sauce over the pieces of chicken.* DINNY *gives* SEAN *the 'thumbs up'.*

(*To* HAYLEY.) Fair dues. You're keeping up so far.

BLAKE *is heard screaming from the smoking wardrobe.*

By jaynee what's this?!

DINNY *races into the sitting room.*

BLAKE, *as his seven-year-old self, appears out of the wardrobe carrying a smouldering stuffed dog with a tent pole up its backside.* SEAN *quickly joins him.*

Speak up and don't be hiding nothing from your daddy.

BLAKE. Minding our own business we were.

SEAN. Big barks and Bouncer hops over the fence like a wild horse.

BLAKE. Wild he is from the pain of the tent pole still up his arse, Dad.

SEAN. It didn't seem right that one of God's animals could be in such torture so Blake made chase.

BLAKE. He took some chasing though. Through the estate and back again.

SEAN. Cornered back in the garden with the pole like a deadly weapon in Bouncer's backside. Into the garden shed he runs. We follow him inside the shed, Dad, and there he lies almost dead, the poor thing.

BLAKE. Pull with all my might and that pole wouldn't budge an inch.

SEAN. Lubrication it needed. Some figure of liquid in a bottle on a shelf I applied to the doggy.

BLAKE. Still not a budge no matter how hard I pulled.

SEAN. He's frozen with the soaking now and Blake tells me to stick his shaking battered body next to the two-bar heater. When BANG!!

BLAKE. He's lit up like a firework all of a sudden! Sure when did Sean ever see methylated spirits, Dad?

SEAN. And when did I hear such screaming from one animal. Flames firing him back on his feet and Bouncer's away like a bat out of hell.

BLAKE. Thankfully the sorry sight came to a stop shortly afterwards.

DINNY. Heart attack, was it?

SEAN. Blake struck him clean with the shovel, Dad.

BLAKE. In fairness he took a few strikes. He was a great little fighter.

DINNY. Good lads.

BLAKE *and* SEAN *exit with the smouldering stuffed dog through the right wardrobe.*

*A pause.*

(*To* HAYLEY.) You didn't see that coming.

HAYLEY. No.

DINNY. Tying up loose ends, teasing out the big finish. (*Shouting.*) Move it, lads! Move it!

SEAN *and* BLAKE *re-enter immediately.* BLAKE *still holds the kitchen knife in his hand and* SEAN *sees this.*

SEAN. Fuck it, he's allowing her to leave, Blake! We can get back to normal! Tell him, Dad!

DINNY (*announcing big*). Maureen, the chicken, love.

SEAN *tries to take the knife off* BLAKE.

SEAN. Please, Blake, no!!

DINNY (*shouts*). Maureen, move it!

HAYLEY *enters still wearing* MAUREEN*'s wig and carrying the chicken on a tray.*

*She looks at* SEAN *but he looks helpless.*

Hang on a sec!

DINNY *takes his moisturiser and whitens* HAYLEY's *face.*

That's more like it. Lovely, Maureen! (*Snaps.*) Kitchen, Sean! Sean as Peter, come on, come on! Poison the lager, sneaky Pete, give it to Jack, do it, do it!

SEAN AS PETER *goes to the kitchen and sees the bucket of 'poison'. He empties some of its contents into a can of beer. He leans over against the sideboard and holds his head momentarily.*

You like the look of your Mammy, Blake.

BLAKE. Yes, Dad. (*Slight pause.*) Scream!

BLAKE *suddenly does a movement where he turns quickly towards the wardrobe and holds his arms above his head. He drops his arms and turns back to the kitchen entrance.*

Scream!

*Again he does the movement. Again he turns back. He's practising something.*

Scream!

*Again the movement.* DINNY *looks on bemused.*

DINNY. Feck it, you're some tulip. (*With energy.*) Chicken everyone?!

BLAKE *takes the tray from* HAYLEY *and indicates for her to return to the kitchen.*

SEAN (*snaps*). Fuck it!

SEAN *quickly opens up a drawer in the kitchen and takes out a knife. He faces the kitchen entrance. He then puts the knife in the pocket of his jacket.*

SEAN AS PETER *appears through the other door, holding the can of 'poisoned' lager as* HAYLEY *enters the kitchen.*

BLAKE AS JACK *snatches the can of beer off* SEAN AS PETER.

BLAKE AS JACK. Cheers, Peter.

SEAN AS PETER. Be my guest.

BLAKE AS VERA (*whispering*). Is that lager poisoned then, Peter?

SEAN AS PETER. The scene's set and soon on a beach we'll lie, Vera.

BLAKE AS JACK. Chicken, Dinny?

DINNY. No chicken for me, Jackie, today's grief has tied my stomach into a tight knot smaller than a gnat's arse.

SEAN AS PADDY. Nor me, Jack. My stomach couldn't handle solids. 'Less you can liquidise that chicken into a savoury shake, it's useless to me.

BLAKE AS JACK. Some of Maureen's special sauce then, Paddy?

SEAN AS PADDY (*eyeing up his can of beer*). There's only one sauce you're holding that interests me.

BLAKE AS JACK *holds the beer out to* SEAN AS PADDY *but, as is his physical catchphrase, pulls it away at the last moment and knocks it back fast.*

Sacriligious, boy. Sacriligious.

BLAKE AS JACK. And finally you Eileen, my wife. A little bit of food needed after the shock of seeing your husband looking so good in a frock?

BLAKE AS EILEEN. It's a whole chicken that's needed, Jack.

BLAKE AS EILEEN *wolfs down a half of chicken.*

BLAKE AS JACK. Eat away, Eileen! Eat away!

BLAKE AS JACK *laughs but suddenly a jolt of pain in his stomach as the poison kicks in. He stares at the can he just drank from.*

(*Groaning.*) I'll be feeling this in the morning.

BLAKE AS JACK *collapses and dies.*

SEAN AS PETER. Let's eat to our bright future so, Vera.

BLAKE AS VERA *is up fast.*

BLAKE AS VERA. Jack dead, then?

SEAN AS PETER. Never again to don the nylons, Vera.

BLAKE AS VERA. Feed us a leg off that chicken so and let us toast our new-found love, Peter!

*A chicken leg each and they feed each other.*

SEAN AS PADDY (*shocked*). What's this, Vera!?

*Suddenly he holds his heart in pain.*

Oh good God no. Not now! Not here!

DINNY. Paddy? Paddy, what is it, little brother?!

SEAN AS PADDY. The wife's turned, Dinny. Turned from me with that knobber Peter and in doing so has fired my fragile hole.

SEAN AS PADDY *drops to his knees.*

It's smaller I'm getting! Smaller!

DINNY. You're on your knees, Paddy.

SEAN AS PADDY. So I am! But sure isn't every Irishman! (*Screams.*) ERIN GO BRAGH!

SEAN AS PADDY *falls over on the floor and dies.*

BLAKE AS VERA. With Paddy the husband gone I'm all yours, Peter love!

BLAKE AS VERA *holds his stomach in pain.*

Oh sweet Jesus! What poisoned trickery is this?

SEAN AS PETER (*holding his stomach in pain*). I fear we've come undone, Vera. Our budding love affair cut short and a shame I'll never get to see you in the nip!

BLAKE AS VERA. Likewise, Peter! It would have been nice to wake up to a virile man as opposed to my Paddy who God bless him was hung like a hamster.

*They both drop to their knees and hold hands.*

*They collapse dead.*

BLAKE *gets up and puts on* EILEEN*'s wig.*

DINNY *looks at* BLAKE AS EILEEN.

DINNY. Eileen, love, don't tell me you had a piece of that poisoned chicken, did ya?

BLAKE AS EILEEN. Never a woman to pass up free grub, Dinny. And never a better man has profited from death. (*Holding his stomach and dropping to his knees.*) The money is all yours! Oh the pain, Dinny, the pain. For me to be cut down in my prime. A woman to be robbed of what the world has to offer! Like a banker without a bank, a journalist without a journal, a painter without paint…

DINNY. All right, Blake!

BLAKE AS EILEEN. Cheerio, oh chosen one.

BLAKE AS EILEEN *dies.*

*A pause.*

DINNY *rushes into the kitchen all excited and starts filling his pockets with Monopoly money.*

SEAN *and* BLAKE *get to their feet and stand opposite each other as they hold their knives in their hands.*

*The two brothers stare at each other as* DINNY *continues inside the kitchen.*

BLAKE. I'm ready to kill her.

SEAN. I won't let you do it, Blake.

BLAKE. A coward like you?!

DINNY (*shouts inside*). Wardrobe, Sean! Move it! SEAN!

BLAKE *grabs* SEAN *and throws him into the wardrobe. He puts a large latch on it to lock* SEAN *inside.*

SEAN (*from inside*). NO!

DINNY (*triumphant*). Well, Maureen, the day of the dead it most certainly is! But even in violent death some glimmer of hope must be sought. Sure aren't people great all the same. A kick in the face and they'll come up smiling. Backs to the wall and it's best foot forward.

DINNY *leaves the kitchen for the sitting room.* HAYLEY *stands at the kitchen door looking at him.*

So away to London I am. Away to treble my new-found wealth and build for us a castle to overlook the English scum. There we'll sit, Maureen, lording over the lot of them, a bit of Cork up there in the sky. It's soon I'll call for you, Maureen. (*Rubbing moisturiser into his face.*) 'Tween now and then keep youthful, love, and I too won't change a jot. Lines won't grow on this face and hair still as thick as a brush, by Christ.

BLAKE AS MAUREEN (*firm*). Yes, Dinny. I'll wait home in Cork for you.

DINNY *throws an arm around* BLAKE *and gives him a little hug. The knife held tight in* BLAKE*'s hand about to strike.*

DINNY. A day of twists and turns and ducks and dives and terrible shocks. A story to be retold, no doubt, and cast in lore. For what are we, Maureen, if we're not our stories?

BLAKE. We're the lost and the lonely.

DINNY. Away to London! Gather around, my little boys! Come and kiss your daddy a final farewell!

BLAKE *fires the knife into* DINNY*'s back.*

DINNY *gasps.* BLAKE *pulls out the knife, turns* DINNY *towards him quickly and stabs him in the stomach hard.*

(*In pain he continues.*) Away… away…

BLAKE (*quietly he prompts him*). 'Away but soon…'

DINNY. Away but soon… Trophy, Blake. Trophy.

BLAKE *hands him his acting trophy.*

BLAKE. 'Away but soon and I'll return to Cork, Maureen.' Say it, Dad.

DINNY *watches the blood pour from his stomach.*

DINNY. Fuck it, that's some acting. Real blood. The blood and bandage, Blake, hah? (*Slight pause*.) Away but soon and I'll return to Cork, Maureen.

DINNY *kisses his trophy.*

HAYLEY *stands in the kitchen entrance petrified.*

BLAKE (*to* HAYLEY). Latch.

HAYLEY *goes to the wardrobe and holds the latch. She looks at* BLAKE.

(*Calmly to* HAYLEY.) Scream.

HAYLEY *screams and opens the latch fast.*

BLAKE *suddenly does the movement where he turns quickly towards the wardrobe and holds his arms above his head.*

SEAN *runs from the wardrobe and drives his knife into* BLAKE's *stomach.*

DINNY *slumps to the ground dead.*

BLAKE *slumps against* SEAN.

*Only now does* SEAN *see his father dead, sees* HAYLEY *alive and realises what his brother has done.*

*He takes the knife out of* BLAKE's *stomach. Blood pours onto the floor.*

BLAKE, *close to death, kisses* SEAN *gently on the lips.*

BLAKE. Now leave, love.

BLAKE *dies.*

*Terrified,* HAYLEY *runs to the front door, scrambles to open the last lock, opens it and exits fast leaving the door open.*

SEAN *lowers* BLAKE *to the floor. He places the knife down on the coffee table. His hand shaking, he takes a drink from a can of beer. He then looks towards the open front door.*

*Reaching under the armchair he takes up the biscuit tin and opens it. He looks inside and takes out a handful of cash. He stands and puts the cash in his pocket.*

*He looks at the tape recorder in front of him. He rewinds the tape. He presses the tape recorder and 'An Irish Lullaby' begins to play.*

*He walks to the front door and stops just inside the flat.*

*He stands there for some time looking out.*

*He then closes the door and begins to lock it.*

*He faces back into the flat.*

*Now quickly and with purpose.* SEAN *resets the coffins, lager, chicken.*

*We watch him quickly move through the main events of the first act.* DINNY *and* PADDY*'s entrance,* VERA *and* MAUREEN*'s entrance, the cheese and crackers on the plate, himself being struck by the frying pan,* JACK *and* PETER*'s entrance,* DINNY *fainting, and finally the Monopoly money being thrown into the air. This all lasts two minutes.*

SEAN *fires a look towards the front door.*

*He walks out to the sitting room.*

*He picks up* HAYLEY*'s coat and puts it on, he lifts up her bag and places it on his shoulder. He takes a plastic Tesco bag from the ground and holds it.*

*He turns his back to us as he stands at the door. He's applying something to his face.*

*'An Irish Lullaby' comes to an end.*

*Silence.*

SEAN *turns. He's covered his face in* DINNY*'s brown shoe polish. He's making* HAYLEY*'s entrance.*

*Loud guttural rhythmic music fades up and fills the stage and auditorium.*

*The light eventually fades down on* SEAN *as we watch him calmly lose himself in a new story.*

*Blackout.*

*Silence.*

*Curtain falls.*

*The End.*

THE NEW ELECTRIC BALLROOM

*The New Electric Ballroom* was first performed by Druid
Theatre Company at the Galway Arts Festival on 14 July 2008,
and later at the Traverse Theatre, Edinburgh, with the following
cast:

| | |
|---|---|
| BREDA | Rosaleen Linehan |
| CLARA | Val Lilley |
| ADA | Catherine Walsh |
| PATSY | Mikel Murfi |
| | |
| *Director* | Enda Walsh |
| *Designer* | Sabine Dargent |
| *Lighting Designer* | Sinéad McKenna |
| *Sound Designer* | Gregory Clarke |

The production was revived on tour in 2009, with Ruth McCabe
playing the role of Clara.

**Characters**

BREDA, *sixties*

CLARA, *sixties*

ADA, *forty*

PATSY, *a fishmonger*

*A living room/kitchen space.*

*On a wall, three different sets of clothes hanging on separate hangers. A cashmere jumper and a rara skirt; a 1950's red blouse and a blue pleated skirt; and a glitzy show-business man's suit.*

*A small kitchen counter with a large delicious-looking sponge cake on it.*

*The atmosphere immediately taut and aggressive.*

*Two older women, in their sixties,* BREDA *and* CLARA, *and a younger one,* ADA, *who is forty.*

CLARA *is sitting.* BREDA *is standing in the corner facing the wall.* ADA *is standing right behind her, staring intently at the back of her head.* ADA *slightly out of breath. She's holding some lipstick in her hand.*

BREDA (*fast and frightened*). By their nature people are talkers. You can't deny that. You could but you'd be affirming what you're trying to argue against and what would the point of that be? No point. Just adding to the sea of words that already exist out there in your effort to say that people are not talkers. But people talk and no one in their right mind would challenge that. Unless you're one of those poor souls starved of vocal cords or that Willy Prendergast boy who used live in town and only managed three words. One was 'yes', one was 'no' and one was 'fish'. Yes yes yes. No no no. Fish fish fish. Fish yes yes. Fish no no. Yes no fish. No yes fish. Fish no fish. Fish yes fish. So even he talked.

CLARA. Look at my little feet.

BREDA. People are born talkers. Those present when a baby comes into the world are made all too aware that the womb is a more desirable place for a baby. That and the unglamorous entrance the baby must make. For all his miracles and great

creations, you'd imagine our Lord could have created a more
dignified point of arrival. This is the man who did wonders
with the mouth and ears and surpassed Himself with the eyes
but sharing a channel with the 'waterworks department'
doesn't strike me as the healthiest environment for a yet-to-
be-born baby and I'm not even a plumber.

CLARA. Would you look at these tiny little hands!

BREDA. People talking just for the act of it. Words spinning to
nothing. For no definable reason. Like a little puppy, a
hungry puppy yapping for his supper, yap-yap-yap-yap…
that's people with words. The breath and the word are
interchangeable. Interchangeable!? Identical. Of course
people breathe to live. While they talk to…

CLARA. I'm getting smaller! I worry too much. Worry does
that, Ada. It does! It stunts you, does worry! Look at the size
of me in this chair. Like a midget!

ADA. You're not a midget.

CLARA. A cup of tea, a cup of tea will sort me out.

BREDA. Won't make you any taller.

CLARA (*snaps*). There's nothing I can't see from here, bitch!

ADA. How could you know that?

CLARA. Instinct.

ADA. Christ…

CLARA. Aren't we ever going to have tea again? Where's
my tea?

ADA (*mimicking*). 'Where's my tea? Where's my tea?'

CLARA. Fetch me my tea, 'Breda the bad girl'.

ADA. There'll be no tea today. (*Turns back and snaps.*) Breda!

BREDA. For that's people with their great need to talk. The
terrible necessity of it. And even besides the talking, far
deeper than the talking, is this need to connect somehow. To
belong. We're out into the world and all is noise and light

and we're speaking of the womb being a more desirable place and it's like the nurse has given us a pill.

CLARA (*mumbles longingly*). Oh, what chance a pill?

BREDA. And the pill gives us this need to belong to 'mother', to 'father', to 'brothers and sisters' and 'in-laws' and 'friends' and 'strangers about to be friends' and 'strangers who'll always be strangers'. The talking is important but superficial really, 'cause the pill gives us a greater compulsion to connect with all these people. To be a part.

CLARA. Fish fish fish! Fish yes fish. No yes fish!

BREDA. But here's the thing…

ADA. Turn around now.

> BREDA *stops and turns around from the corner and faces* ADA. *Her face is aggressively marked with red lipstick, we guess that it's been done by* ADA. BREDA *holds a ceramic kitchen bowl. Seeing her,* CLARA, *frightened, covers her eyes.*

(*Quietly prompting.*) Wherever…

*A slight pause.*

BREDA. Wherever that pill resides in the body it doesn't reach the further recesses of the brain. 'Cause sitting back there… back there and likely only to make the odd appearance, is the 'hard truth'…

ADA. Slow.

*A pause.*

BREDA (*slower*). And the 'hard truth' reminds us that we'll always be alone, baby sister. Besides the yap-yap and the arms outstretched and our great compulsion to be with others, we'll always be back in the womb. Back there and reminding ourselves that the womb is a more desirable place than this 'created world'. We don't want to be alone but we're alone. We don't want to be an island but we are that island.

*A pause.*

Will I put the piece of paper back in its bowl, Ada?

*She does so and* ADA *takes the bowl off her.*

ADA (*to* BREDA). Is it true we're alone?

BREDA *nods.*

Us more than anyone else?

BREDA. The same.

BREDA *touches her nose. Blood spills down her face.* ADA *just looks at her.*

CLARA (*announcing*). Nobody… Makes… Cake… Like… You… Clara.

BREDA *goes to sit down.*

Our mother would always say that. She said I was a born baker. She said I had a gift for coffee cake the way Jesus had a gift for sacrifice. When I was six she'd place me on her lap and I'd mix the flour with the eggs and the sugar and the coffee. And we'd be half-listening to the radio and her leg would send me up and down like I'm on a horse trotting. Not galloping now! Never a gallop. She'd get me to recite the alphabet while the cake stretched out in the heat inside. The lovely pattern of the ABCs over and over as it pumps the air into the sponge. Me and the oven in happy unison, in lovely poetry. Sure, look at the consistency of that sponge cake!

BREDA. Enough, Clara!

BREDA *stares over at* ADA *who is lost in her thoughts.* BREDA *starts removing the lipstick from her face with some baby wipes.*

CLARA. If it was entered into a contest… imagine the envy. Imagine all those old bitches hiding their hate because of my prize. A local photographer is there and their faces looking up at me, Ada. The girls from the cannery looking at me! At me! And I turn to Holy Mary, 'cause she's standing there right beside, and the mother of Jesus takes me aside and says, 'You're the best, Clara. Better than all them who locked you inside. Who spun out the gossip in the cannery and locked that door behind you. You're better than all those bitches.'

BREDA. Clara!

CLARA. So I slice off a piece of cake for the mother of Jesus… and she scoffs it down, not in the least bit like a virgin, but what do you expect, what with the great divinity of this sponge? What colour rosette would they give me for winning with such a great coffee cake? There's too many colours to choose from. What heavenly colour, Ada?

*A very long pause.*

There's a terrible lull in the conversation. The sort of lull that can get you worrying about other things.

*A pause.*

Will I take the piece of paper from the bowl, Ada?

ADA *doesn't answer.*

Can we not have a cup of tea and some of that lovely coffee cake I made?

*A pause.*

BREDA (*to* ADA). Did something happen outside, pet?

*A long pause.*

ADA. The town still asleep I cycle to work as always. Through the little narrow streets and over the cobblestones away from the sea and towards the cannery up on the hill. I see a furniture van outside Mrs Cullen's house. She's getting a new kitchen put in and her stood watching the men carrying the fancy cabinets through her garden and into her house. Her little dog Bobby's bouncing up and down and yapping the way little dogs do. I can see her looking at me as I pass by and a coldness in her face because of what us three are to them. I cycle on and into the cannery and walk through the floor with the loud machines tinning the fish… still echoing with the gossip of Clara and Breda and the Roller Royle. Into my little office and head down and lost in the numbers and turning fish into money. Just me and the machines. No one but me and the sea being tinned. (*Slight pause*.) It's evening and I cycle home and the streets are again empty and that furniture van passes and gets me thinking of Mrs Cullen's new fitted kitchen and for some reason I stop my bike outside her house. And I'm standing there imagining her in a yellow light surrounded by all her new things. (*Pause*.) He's lying on the ground dying. His insides are more out than in. His blond hair stuck with blood and bits. I can see the whole scene played out. The kitchen fitted and Mrs Cullen inside and Bobby bouncing up and down and yapping at the men as they get into the van. And the van pulls away and Bobby closer and closer still and caught under the wheel and laid into the road. I'm seeing all of this played out with Mrs Cullen at her door and walking towards me and then seeing Bobby lying on the road and then bent over getting sick into her begonias… and she's crying now… she's crying. (*Pause*.) I'm standing with my bicycle watching and…!! I start to smile. I'm smiling at a woman and her dying dog and Christ it's like a bullet through me then. (*Slight pause*.) How is it I've come to feel this way?

*A door opens. It's* PATSY *the fishmonger with a plastic tray full of large fish.*

PATSY. All right, the ladies?

BREDA. Leave them where you stand and go.

PATSY *puts down the tray.*

PATSY. Terrific news about Nana Cotter, isn't it? A hundred years, God bless her, and a lovely letter from the President of congratulations.

*A pause as the sisters don't answer.*

To mark the occasion she got her hair done in a purple rinse and a party was thrown with all manner of vol-au-vents and trifle present.

*A pause as the sisters remain silent.*

Poor love got a little excited and shit herself…

CLARA. Would you look at these tiny little feet!

PATSY. Yeah, she's a great woman, Nana, all right. Little bones like summer kindling, hands like pigeon's feet, hearing shot from years of working in the cannery but by Jesus can she eat trifle? Eat it? Like a Hoover!

*A pause. He doesn't want to leave, despite it being obvious he's an unwelcome guest.*

Mr Simmons got his hip done. Looks a hell of lot more normal than before. Great to see him back all level. He's a sprightly ninety-year-old, despite all his misfortunes. Feck it, he's had that many trips to the garage, he's more plastic than flesh, but to see his little cataract eyes lit up with renewed life…

BREDA. You can go now, we're busy.

PATSY. But what a lovely smell of coffee cake in here. Different houses have their own stamp. I could close my eyes and still make my way around town if the front doors were open. I'd be the first to say I'm not the sharpest knife in the rack and I'm no looker either. People have said I have the looks of a man who's been struck in the face by a wet fish and I couldn't argue with that for the truth is I have often been struck by a wet fish in the face. Several times in fact. But when it comes to smelling things… well, boys!! You won't find a keener nose in the whole of the county! Obviously some people think that's an unfortunate ability, what with me being a fishmonger, and they wouldn't be wrong…

CLARA (*blocks her ears and mumbles*). Yes no no! No yes fish! Fish fish fish…

PATSY. But God, that was a great night the other night! Mags Donald had all her grandchildren in the pub and while I was only passing through to use the gents I had to stop a while and listen to the great sing-along. Like a lark her little crippled grandson sang and we were all reduced to tears when Mags got up and said what a gift from God this little spastic was. But feck it, what breeding! Like their own village they were. Masses of them spread around her feet like Mags herself was giving a sermon at the Mount and though no loaves and fishes were present there was plenty of crisps and scampi…

BREDA (*snaps*). What is it, Patsy!?

*A pause. Again he looks towards the open door and then back.*

PATSY. Things are odd. (*Slight pause.*) Outside.

BREDA. Tell him stop, Ada!

ADA *lowers her head.*

Leave!

PATSY. I'm standing in the little shoebox I call my bedroom, Ada. I'm standing in my underpants. I'm standing there staring down on my little bed, the sheets all creased and…? Like skin. The pillow dented from where I lay my head. The shape of me marked out on the bed, mapping out my night's sleep. And for some reason that gets me nervous so that I have to leave the room. The house quiet as always. The little stairs groaning as always. Everything as always but for this ball of butterflies growing inside me. So I dress real quick and leave and off and out to work. I'm outside then. And the narrow cobbled streets of the town are a bit uneasy underfoot. The narrow streets narrower somehow. The houses on either side, they're leaning in that bit close to me. They're squeezing me, hurrying me towards work. I come to the little harbour to gather up my fish from the boats like I always do. I say hello to Simple Paddy who helps out in the harbour tying up the boats. I listen to his dream from the night before, the way I always do listen. It takes some listening because of his cleft palate but I listen all the same. Anyway I'm being smacked with that much spit that I have to look away. And I see over his shoulder that the seas are getting smaller. They're getting smaller. I look up to the cliffs and it really looks like the cliffs are receding. Can sort of feel the seas and cliffs being drawn back in and disappearing and becoming butterflies inside me. I have that feeling that today will be the start of my last day. (*He covers his eyes.*) I can see a picture of me running from your house.

My heart's been ripped out and the ground underneath is loose underfoot. I'm running towards the harbour from this cliff. I can see the harbour being sucked into the sand and the cliffs pulled back like you would pull a curtain back. There's a great space now with me running over it towards nothing, towards…! No place. My heart's been ripped out, yet I can't stop running.

*A pause. He lowers his hands from his eyes.*

I can see all this… and then I'm back on the harbour with Simple Paddy and his cleft palate spitting over me.

*A pause.*

ADA. From this house you ran?

PATSY. Yes, Ada, from here.

BREDA. Leave, Patsy!

PATSY *leaves with* BREDA *slamming the door closed behind him.*

Why is it you allowed him to talk like that!?

ADA *marches over to a small table where an old tape recorder stands.*

ADA (*snaps*). Quiet!

ADA *rewinds a tape.*

CLARA. It's time, then.

CLARA *stands and she and* BREDA *watch* ADA*'s every move.*

Won't you say who it is, Ada, please? Is it Breda the bad girl?

*The tape stops.* ADA *presses the play button and what begins is a foley soundtrack roughly pasted together by* ADA *to accompany the story we're about to hear.*

ADA. It's time and looking in the mirror and this feeling of everything not too right…

CLARA. Whose story, Ada?

ADA. It's time and looking in the mirror and this feeling…

CLARA. Ada?

ADA. …of everything not too right, not too right. Up in the bathroom and my eighteen-year-old body…

CLARA. …tries to shake off these…

ADA. Louder!

CLARA. …tries to shake off these…

ADA. Louder, Clara!

CLARA. …tries to shake off these doubts. Staring back behind the blusher and eyeshadow a girl who's yet to be kissed. Properly kissed.

ADA. Been mauled in the car park…

CLARA. Been mauled in the car park once outside The Sunshine Ballroom. Mauled by Jimbo 'The Face' Byrne, a fisherman stinking of stout and mackerel with the biggest face in the west. Crushed me up against his Ford Cortina and tore at my tits. Jimbo's head like an old horse all stooped and drunk. His fish fingers like hooks on my good blouse. But never been properly kissed…

ADA. But thoughts of him…

CLARA. Yes, thoughts of 'him' have me more forward thinking.

BREDA *starts to undress* CLARA *down to her slip.*

ADA. Louder.

CLARA. Thoughts of 'him' have me more forward thinking. For weren't they his words that asked me to meet him backstage? Wasn't it him that placed us together with that promise…

ADA. You meet me after.

CLARA. 'You meet me after.' And butterflies carry me down stairs. The soles of my feet tingling 'cause of 'him'. The top of my head all fizz! It's my time. It's my time.

ADA. You smell nice.

CLARA. Dad's voice stuck behind the newspaper and I tuck into my Saturday fry.

The rustling newspaper has me in mind of the crowd that'll gather tonight.

ADA. You meet me after.

CLARA. Packed so tight and faced towards the stage, we are. Clothes sparking off each other, shined leather shoes sticking on the dance floor. The chatter loud so you can't hear words and only these crackling noises. I polish off the bacon in double-quick time!

ADA *and* BREDA *grunt like pigs.*

ADA. Do it!

CLARA *grunts like a pig, joining* ADA *and* BREDA *in the grunting.*

BREDA *nonchalantly walks to the wall and takes down the 1950's rara skirt and the cashmere jumper.*

ADA *stops grunting.*

Sweet Breda.

CLARA. And through the door and Breda too made-up for the dance. Made-up in her nice blue skirt and red blouse… (*Suddenly forgets.*)

ADA. Her silent as usual! Mother slides…

CLARA. What?

ADA. Her silent as usual!

CLARA. Her silent as usual. Mother slides her fry towards her and like a little bird, her bites of the bacon. Like a little birdy! The rustling of the newspaper and her little lady bites. Her little lady bites. Her little lady bites! (*Mimics the birdlike noises and bites of* BREDA. *Snaps.*) 'Can't you eat like a humanfuckingbeing?!'

BREDA *starts dressing* CLARA *in the rara skirt and cashmere jumper.*

ADA. Time to leave…

CLARA. …and each on our bike with the ten-mile cycle to The New Electric Ballroom spread out ahead like a yellow-brick road.

ADA. The town behind…

CLARA. …and the cobblestone streets sewing it up all neat and perched by the sea, ahh look. We're away, Breda and me, with the… (*Again she's forgotten.*) With the…?

ADA. …with the old road steering…

CLARA (*breaking down*). I can't…

ADA. …with the old road steering us towards The New Electric.

CLARA. Breda, please…

ADA *grabs* CLARA *hard.* ADA *continues the story by herself.*

ADA. And move through the evening with pleated skirts hiding the busy legs beneath. They hide the things that want to be touched by him. They cover all desire and yet smouldering with each yard cycled. The breaths shorter, the freshly pressed blouses a little damp from the sweat. The make-up hot so that the face shimmers. So far behind The Sunshine Ballroom of our poxy harbour town and its lonely fishermen.

BREDA *applies make-up to* CLARA*'s face.*

Them fishermen mauling us like we're the fecking fish. Closing in on us, closing up the dance floor and backed into the corners 'til it's one on one. The lust in their faces. The heavy pants and sweaty palms. Their excuse for dancing? This rhythmless jumping up and down like they've just shit themselves. Which they have. Which they have! How they've trapped our little town in the Stone Age. Perched by the sea, this town needs drowning and reborn. (*Snaps.*) Clara!

CLARA. We cycle on, losing the memory of The Sunshine for The New Electric. The dusty road beneath turning to tarmacadam and the bigger town. The pace kicking us off our bicycles and how we now walk in this new town. Pushing out our little tits with a new confidence now. An American confidence!

ADA. That promise of…

CLARA. 'You meet me after.' His words have me queuing up outside The New Electric and pressed up against its wall.

ADA. Take a breath.

CLARA. For fear I'll blow up, a breath now, Clara.

*A pause as* CLARA *breathes and gathers herself.*

ADA. Slower.

CLARA (*slower now*). So leaned against the wall. Still have that little girl inside me.

I'm still sat on Mother's knee with hands all flour and cake. I'm still young enough to think of the world as family and town only. I'm at this moment. I'm at the edge of what it is to be a woman. I look from the corner and see all that I'm stepping into, like I'm moving from the black and white to the Technicolor. From nights mauled by fishermen to moments of wanted passion. Behind this wall… his words and desire and my new feelings of…

ADA (*faster now*). And enter then…

CLARA. And enter then…

ADA. And enter then…

CLARA. And enter…

*Sounds of a dance floor and music played louder by* ADA.

…and all is bodies. Bodies stuck together by numbers and sweat and music and beats and dance and cigarette smoke. And armless, legless bodies held up in a sea of skinny men in dark suits and young women's floral skirts. Already moving in a tide of badly suppressed sex… Oh, we move…

ADA. And Breda…

CLARA. …and Breda…? And Breda then separated, thank
Christ. My last tie to home and the life before and Breda's
ambition stuck… stuck in the cloakroom and soaked in
mineral orange, the sap! Well, not me. Not Clara. Me, passed
from stream to stream…

ADA. Louder!

CLARA. Me, passed from stream to stream and nearing the
stage with lungs squeezed so tight. A mixture of torture and
foreplay I can hear his voice crushing women's hearts and
winning the admiration of any man with manhood but not
quite the time to open my eyes to my man on stage. (*Slight
pause*.) But open then… and there he is! 'The Roller Royle'
and his showband. His stance… All-American. His suit a
shade of blue right out of summer. His quiff, with no respect
to gravity, whipped up on his head and reaching skywards.
The Roller Royle. I hear his words from four weeks ago and
my heart skips, my breath stops, my head races. 'You meet
me after. You meet me after…'

BREDA. Done.

*BREDA is finished and CLARA has been fully transformed
to her eighteen-year-old self.*

Well?

ADA (*nods*). Very good.

*BREDA sits and looks at the scene as it continues.*

CLARA. So afterwards then…

ADA. Wait, Clara!

*ADA then turns off the lights so that a single light isolates
CLARA in the space.*

Afterwards…

CLARA. And backstage and pointed to where the Roller waits.
Can hear his hit single, 'Wondrous Place', reel me in, his
lovely voice soothing me and making this nervous scene a

little easier. The corridor busy with people packing up and moving on to the next town but all thoughts are of him, Ada. Him and the things we will do together. Near his dressing room and my heart slower, my future mapped out with mornings met by his face and his sweet voice singing about this oh-so-wondrous place. The door a little open…

I enter.

*A pause. Suddenly* CLARA *gasps for air and her eyes fill with tears.*

He's sat on a table with you stood between his legs. (*Pause.*) He has his face tucked into you. (*Pause.*) His big hands around your tiny waist and he's kissing your mouth.

CLARA *looks to* BREDA.

My throat's jammed with those butterflies. My blood pumped slower. My heart shot all in an instant. It's your blue skirt and red blouse, Breda the bad girl. (*Slight pause.*) I can feel the hooked fingers of Jimbo 'The Face' Byrne tear at my blouse and rip out my heart and claim it as his. I'm stood still… but I'm already running through The New Electric, already travelling the ten miles home and with each yard putting an end to any thoughts of love. Each yard travelled and more distance between me and any wish for what is… (*Almost spits.*) This love. The wind is on my back, and the tide is inching in and the cobblestones uneasy. The winding streets of our harbour town twisting me to the inside. The narrow streets narrower somehow. The houses on either side leaning in too close to me. Telling me, squeezing me, hurrying me towards my inside. Inside where's safe. Get inside, Clara. Get inside. Get inside. Get inside. Get inside…

ADA *turns* CLARA *towards her and stares at her.* ADA *turns the tape recorder off. She then goes and switches the lights back on. She goes to the kitchen cupboard and opens it. Inside, the cupboard is packed with the same type of plain biscuits. She takes out one packet. She hands* CLARA *a biscuit.*

I'm finished for now?

ADA *nods and then gently pats her on the head.*

Will I not have the nice coffee cake I made?

ADA *hands* BREDA *a biscuit.*

Will I not have some tea to wash down this biscuit, Ada?

*A long pause.* ADA *looks around the space and then at her two sisters eating the plain biscuits. Suddenly, she fires the packet of biscuits against the front door. Biscuits fly everywhere.*

*The front door opens. It's* PATSY *with another plastic tray full of large fish.*

PATSY. All right, the ladies?

BREDA. Leave them where you stand and go.

*PATSY puts down the tray.* BREDA *goes about cleaning up the biscuits.*

PATSY. Great to see Mary Calley fighting fit after her fall outside Bingo. I heard she had a few to drink and that would account for the terrible thump she gave the ground.

Popped her kneecap right open...

CLARA. That's enough, Patsy.

PATSY. She'll be using the walking stick for another month but that wouldn't put her out much. She only ever does two things as far as I can see, the pub and the Bingo and both of them involve sitting...

BREDA. Patsy!

PATSY. But you'd have to wonder the effects that concentration on a bingo sheet with a stomach full of Malibu has on your average seventy-year-old. That's the thing with age, you see. Medicine is well on top of its treatment to many people but the body of a pensioner is a bit of a lucky bag, isn't it? A routine treatment can uncover all manner of hidden diseases and random ailments. Phyllis Ryan went to the doctor's to get him to move his car and walked away with a burst appendix! I mean, that's a cruel lottery...

BREDA. Leave!

PATSY. Yes, Breda…

BREDA. Now, Patsy, that's enough!

PATSY. Out the door, out the door now, Breda!

PATSY *looks towards the open door. Again, he looks very anxious. He can't leave.*

*Frustrated, he stamps on the ground hard.*

SHITE!

*The sisters don't react.* PATSY *then punches himself hard in the stomach. Again the sisters don't react. Again he punches his stomach hard. Again no reaction.*

*A very long pause.*

PATSY. I saw Bernie Doyle in her front garden with all her grandchildren having a picnic and I've never seen such an amount of jelly in all my life. Mountains of it. (*Slight pause.*) I shouldn't have been there, I know that now. I shouldn't have. Sometimes my body has a will of its own and I find myself walking the little streets with no destination in mind. THESE BLOODY LEGS! (*Slight pause.*) I was across the road standing on the path and looking at the picnic and it was a lovely scene and her son, Bernie's son, he's a fisherman and his name is Finbarr, well, he's there with his lovely wife and his two kids and I shouldn't have done it, ladies, I know I shouldn't have done it, I shouldn't have done it!… but I started to imagine me as Finbarr. Me on his great big trawler out on the seas… though I wouldn't last a day on account of me getting seasick all the time… but I'm thinking about what it'd be like to have a meal with his lovely wife. What fish we'd order. I'm thinking in great detail then. Well, feck it, I stop all those thoughts 'cause it's cruel to me and to an outsider it's a bit creepy, so I give myself a good kick in the hole and I go to my dancing lessons in Sheila and Robert's house high on the hill, in their lovely sitting room with their paintings on the wall of exotic islands they've never visited. The waltzes and tangos and foxtrots and rumbas and we're

learning the salsa at the moment and that's a great laugh, all
right! Because there's only the three of us, and Sheila and
Robert are a couple, I don't get to practise with another, so
I'm just sitting there in their lovely sitting room and
watching them dance and I start to think about Finbarr and
his wife again. 'Stop it, Patsy, that's enough! STOP IT
NOW!'(*Slight pause*.) And... And then suddenly I get this
big hole in my stomach. The sort of hole you might fall into.
And the more I look at Sheila and Robert and think of
Finbarr and his wife, it feels like the walls of this hole are
being scooped out by needles so that I'm doubled over in the
armchair. And Robert's standing over me with my mouth all
twisting from the pain of these needles, you see.... and feck
it, I get up fast and leave and I'm walking the cobblestones
and right above me are the seagulls gathering and they're
sort of laughing at me 'cause I'm holding my stomach and
doubled over. And it's tearing inside and with each second I
get glimpses of me alone. Me in the bed... alone. Me on the
streets... alone. Me staring at the cliffs receding... alone. At
the beginning the seagulls are laughing. My walk quickens
with the fucking seagulls following me and having a laugh.
And then I hear one of them say, 'What is the purpose of
you, Patsy? What is the purpose of you?' Well, I start to run
now, 'cause that's a very hard question to answer and even
harder when it's been asked by a bloody seagull! A seagull
who's got the wings and the where-for-all to get the fuck out
of town and fly off to somewhere else. What is the purpose
of me? Too big a question. Run on, Patsy! And Mary
Calley's looking from the pub with her busted leg put out on
the table. And she sees me running past and her eyes all big
then, her gob already wagging and spreading the gossip
about 'Patsy the mad fishmonger', the bitch! Well, what 'as
she got to gossip about when there's that amount of Malibu
in her she's like her very own Caribbean island! Run on
then! Run on! Run run run run! (*Pause*.) I stop and I'm
standing at your door with these fish again. Look behind and
see the cliffs receding. The seas being sucked back into the
sand. The tides toing and froing all confused and restless...
no sense to them. No sense to time. I'm back again at your
door. (*Slight pause*.) Well, I start to think and try to get at

least one thing clear. (*Pause*.) The only thing that is certain in my life is that I always come to this house. I come with the tide, don't I? And that is a certainty... and that certainty, it soothes me, somehow. It keeps the bigger question of 'purpose' at bay. It mightn't stop the seas shrinking or the cliffs receding but, that certainty, it does... soothe me.

*A pause. The sisters remain quiet. Perhaps they're not even listening.*

And before now I have never asked for anything. I have never asked why for all these years you've stayed inside, Clara and Breda. I don't ask that question for really I have no business asking. But if coming here is my only certainty and I have the same rhythm as these tides... I wonder now if you ladies would open up to me a little and treat me as a visitor some day. Have a good word to say to me even.

BREDA. Go.

PATSY. I won't return 'less I have a kind word.

BREDA. Don't be stupid, you'll return with the tide.

PATSY. But for what greater purpose?

BREDA. Leave.

PATSY. What purpose, Ada?!

*ADA walks over and holds the door for him.*

Ada?

*Slight pause.*

ADA. To bring the fish.

*PATSY leaves, ADA slamming the door closed behind him.*

*CLARA and BREDA go and place each tray of fish in a large chute in the wall as ADA stands, lost in her thoughts, looking at the front door.*

*ADA then opens the front door slowly and looks out.*

*BREDA, concerned, looks at ADA. CLARA stands looking at the cake.*

CLARA. She never did age, the Virgin Mary. You might put that down to the Middle-Eastern cuisine but Mary Magdalene had a face like a saddle and the truth is, a whore ages worse than someone clean.

BREDA. Clara!

CLARA (*sighs*). Will we ever eat this cake?

BREDA *increasingly concerned over* ADA*'s behaviour.*

ADA *remains looking out the front door at the outside as a beautiful golden light slowly fades up outside.*

ADA. I'm sitting in my office floating over the accounts changing fish into numbers.

Seconds and minutes are marking out time but it's the numbers that are marking me out. Making the rhythm of me, balancing me. I look up from the numbers and into the pattern of the day we've made here in this house. When I step out of the office I should be on my way home to your stories and the tea and the cake and Patsy and his fish... But I've stepped on to a beach and my very own new story now. And the sand's like cotton wool underfoot and when I look down the sand's golden. And the air all about me is warm, so it cannot be this island here. And no narrow streets and strange tides and talking seagulls... here the horizon open and light. There's a calm about me because the day has possibilities. And I'm calm because of that.

*She covers her eyes with her hand.*

But the sea is too still and there's no wind whatsoever and the clouds above are still. Nothing's moving because nothing's real. Like I'm standing in a picture of a beach and not the beach itself. A little child runs past. A six-year-old and I recognise her face when she turns around and smiles. I've seen her in old photographs and I know I'm looking at me running up this beach. She's the girl before you taught me these stories. (*Slight pause.*) I'm looking at her lying face down in a rock pool. I'm pulling her by the hair out of the water.

*A pause. She lowers her hand from her eyes.*

Things can never change here, can they?

CLARA *and* BREDA *remain silent.*

I really have to leave.

BREDA *walks intently towards the small table where the old tape recorder stands. She starts rewinding the tape.* ADA *turns and looks at her.*

CLARA (*rubbing her hands together, all excited*). It's time! It's time!

ADA. Stop it, Breda!

*The tape stops.* CLARA *has gone to the door and slams it shut.*

BREDA *presses the play button and what begins is the same soundtrack by* ADA *to accompany the stories.*

BREDA. It's time and looking in the mirror and this feeling of everything not too right. Up in the bedroom and my seventeen-year-old body tries to shake off these doubts. Staring back behind the blusher and eyeshadow a girl who's already been kissed. Been properly kissed. Was it only four weeks ago in the car park outside The New Electric?

CLARA *starts undressing* BREDA *down to her slip.*

I was stood looking at the ground and every detail of that spot... the split tarmacadam, a plume of clover, its close proximity to the chip van... his hand in mine. The details. The Roller Royle. His hand on my waist and his words.

ADA *confused that it is* BREDA *leading the story.*

ADA. Breda, we don't...

BREDA. The details. The Roller Royle. His hand on my waist and his words...

ADA. Stop...

BREDA (*screams*). SAY IT!!

*A slight pause.*

ADA (*subdued*). 'We'll do it the next…'

BREDA. 'We'll do it the next time, Breda.' Little kiss then. Nothing too animal, more of a Gregory Peck. Turns away with his chips and my heart and into their van. Four weeks then. Four weeks 'til the next time, my first time.

CLARA *takes the 1950's blue pleated skirt and red blouse from the wall.*

ADA (*distant*). Mother calls…

BREDA. And down the stairs on butterflies and into the kitchen and Dad hidden behind the newspaper and the pig face of Clara at her bacon like a dog. The sad hateful face of my sister done up like a clown. How the other girls in the cannery laugh at her behind her stumpy back. Clara, dragging the family down with her mournful eyes and doughy skin. Take to my fry like a bird with my stomach churning with thoughts of the Roller Royle. Perfumed my bra and knickers in anticipation. Stood at the mirror that morning and slid my hands down my pants. Had a chit-chat conversation with myself as him, and took my hands to the rest of me. But tonight's the night. And each on our bike with the ten-mile cycle to The New Electric spread out ahead like a yellow-brick road. The town behind and the cobblestone streets sewing it up all neat and perched by the sea. Well, good enough for drowning and little else! Cycle on and on and feel like one of those Greek heroes taking to the seas, escaping into something better than the poxy Sunshine Ballroom with its oh-so-sad fishermen!

ADA. Buy you a mineral, Breda? Have a biscuit in the car park with me, Breda! (*Chants.*) Breda, Breda, Breda, Breda!

BREDA. And did once with Jimbo 'The Face' Byrne… a man with the biggest face in the west. Handed me his custard cream and asked me to lick the cream from the biscuit. Did so and saw him beating himself off, leaned against his Ford Cortina.

ADA. And enter then…

BREDA. And enter then…

ADA. And enter then…

BREDA. And enter…

*Sounds of a dance floor and music played louder by* ADA *as* CLARA *adds make-up to* BREDA*'s face.*

And all is bodies.

ADA. Louder!

BREDA. And all is bodies…

ADA. Bodies stuck together by numbers and sweat and music and beats and dance and cigarette smoke. And Clara then separated. My last tie to home shunted from my back and Clara's ambition stuck in the Hucklebuck with some sad someone else! But not Breda.

BREDA. Well, not me, lads. Not me. Me already steered towards the backstage. Steered as the Roller Royle serenades his Faithful. The women who'd gladly go all the way and the young men aping the great man himself.

ADA. Backstage…

BREDA. And the showband out front keeping time with my wanting heart. Into the Roller's dressing room and my skin is not my own. All alive it is! Tingling with images and giddy on love! Must settle for fear I blow up… and I do so… I do settle. Settle.

Settle. Settle, Breda. (*Slight pause.*) I start to think of me as a girl. Seventeen and I'm at the edge of things now. Leave behind the safety of all before…

ADA. Leave behind the safety of my home and our little town and step into the real world with love as my only guide.

BREDA *looks at* ADA.

With real love, Breda. Do you understand me?

BREDA *slaps* ADA *hard across the face.* ADA *shaken.*

BREDA *continues.*

BREDA. I can hear the band finishing up with 'Wondrous Place' and for a heartbeat... doubts raise their head. (*Slight pause*.) Door opens and there he is. Words are passed but to no point, no reason. The little room all charged with me and him... so no room for the words as he sits on a table and calls me over. I hold my head back, open my mouth a little and he kisses me softly. His fingers find their way down my back and slide into my pleated skirt and then round front 'til it stops on my belly. Tongues deeper and he lowers his hand then. Lowers it so it's in the perfumed knickers and I push into his hand. And I'm thinking I am his. He is mine certainly. His finger deeper and no doubts now. I can feel him through his pants and I know it's my time. I'm here at the start of a new life and it's my time. Door slams...

CLARA. ...and someone there but gone.

BREDA. 'Stay put, I'll be back, I'll be back, Breda!' (*Quietly*.) Yes.

CLARA *is finished changing* BREDA *into her seventeen-year-old self. She's squeezed into her blouse and skirt.*

CLARA *then hands* BREDA *the show-business suit from the wall.*

CLARA *turns off the lights but for the single light which isolates* BREDA.

BREDA *is suddenly overcome and her eyes fill with tears.* ADA *instinctively takes advantage then.*

ADA (*snaps*). Breda! (*Prompting her.*) Outside then!

BREDA *slowly shakes her head.*

BREDA (*quietly*). I can't.

ADA *goes to her, grabs her by the shoulders and starts shaking her violently.*

ADA. Outside!

ADA *stops.* BREDA *must continue until the end.*

BREDA. Outside and the moon lighting up the scene teasing me more. I can see him walking towards a new face standing in the same spot where I stood. That plume of clover just beneath her in the split tarmacadam. Her…? All Doris Day-like, all sweetness. He's moving in. I can see his big hand on her tiny waist. I can see him mouth the words… 'It's your time…' and little Doris folding into him now. (*Slowly.*) I'm standing, hugging his suit, Ada. My insides start retching. My mouth that he kissed all sour now, where he touched all muck. I'm still but already travelling the ten miles home and with each yard putting an end to any thoughts of love. Each yard travelled and more distance between me and any wish for what it is to be in love. And the wind is on my back and his song mocking me. And the narrow streets of our town they're narrower somehow. The houses on either side leaning in that bit close to me. They're squeezing me, hurrying me towards the inside of this house. To get inside. And stay inside always and keep safe away from this wondrous place. Keep safe. Keep safe inside always.

ADA *turns off the tape and* CLARA *switches back on the lights.*

*A long pause.* ADA *stares at* BREDA *who stands, alone and beaten.*

ADA. I'm only a baby when I first hear that story from you, Breda. Then thousands of times I've made you tell it again and again like some child… though I am not a child. (*Pause.*) Still, it hurts you just the same, isn't that right?

BREDA. Isn't this what we've tried to teach you? (*Slight pause.*) Don't you feel safer inside than out?

*A slight pause.*

ADA. I don't feel anything.

ADA *looks towards the front door.*

CLARA *stands looking at the cake again.*

CLARA. What would the Virgin Mary make of all of this, I wonder? Like many women I'd say she keeps an ordered house, but surely she'd have cause to worry for us three. I can almost feel my brain getting softer and it certainly feels like a nearer paradise.

Yes.

*A slight pause.*

(*Sighs.*) Will we ever eat this cake?

BREDA (*to* ADA). It's time for your rest and then we'll start over.

ADA *nods that she understands. She goes to a room and sits wide awake on the bed.*

BREDA *places the suit back on the wall. A long pause.*

CLARA. There's a lull. Sort of lull that can get you worried. Pass me the bowl, it's time!

BREDA *holds the bowl to her and* CLARA *puts her hand into it. She's very excited. She picks out the one folded up piece of paper that's in there. She unwraps it and reads.*

(*Surprised.*) 'No man is an island'!

BREDA *turns over an hourglass.*

BREDA. Begin.

BREDA *begins to take off her 'costume'.*

CLARA. By their nature people are talkers. You can't deny that. You could but you'd be affirming what you're trying to argue against and what would the point of that be? No point. Just adding to the sea of words that already exist out there in your effort to say that people are not talkers. But people talk and no one in their right mind would challenge that. Unless you're one of those poor souls starved of vocal cords or that Willy Prendergast boy who used live in town and only managed three words. One was 'yes', one was 'no' and one was 'fish'. But even he talked. People are born talkers. Those present when a baby comes into the world are made all too aware that the womb is a more desirable place for a baby. That and the unglamorous entrance the baby must make. For all his miracles and great creations, you'd imagine our Lord could have created a more dignified point of arrival. This is the man who did wonders with the mouth and ears and surpassed Himself with the eyes but sharing a channel with the 'waterworks department' doesn't strike me as the healthiest environment for a yet-to-be-born baby. And I'm not even a plumber. But people get set in their ways early on. Spat out into the world with this feeling of superiority, some people! Stuck in the pram and already the prime spot! Sat opposite me and already the pristine doll…

BREDA. Stuck in the pram, the lumpen pig. Sat opposite me, Mother's little gargoyle…

CLARA. I'm standing looking at your underwear laid out on the bed. I can smell the perfume and it's you who sends me off to the bathroom with a stomach full of doubts!

BREDA. On with the underwear and already you sitting there on my back. Stuck there with your face the picture of this town. The happy pig at the trough with your thoughts of The Sunshine Ballroom. Taking the biscuit in the car park, hey, Clara?! Opening your zip for Jimbo 'The Face'. (*Chants.*) Clara, Clara, Clara, Clara!

CLARA. And cycling the ten miles to The New Electric and you as always po-faced. Like a big plank there! A long streak of misery. Off the bike with tits out and how they look at you, these boys… such indifference.

BREDA. Off the bike and sweat clinging to your hairy back. You smelling like a damp April day though everywhere else is summer. Stood in the queue and again I've got you staining my style. You with your slap-happy face and doughy body stood outside The New Electric like a dressed-up Neanderthal…

CLARA. And enter then…

BREDA. And enter then…

CLARA. And enter then…

BREDA. And enter and get busy throwing you off my back…

CLARA. Throwing you off my back!

BREDA. And 'Wondrous Place' and seconds away from your big heartache.

CLARA. You and the Roller. The big romantic scene…

BREDA. And his hand on my back, and his hand down my front, and his mouth against my mouth. While you're stood there with that face collapsing into tears…

CLARA. And you stood outside in the car park with your sodden perfumed knickers, your stony face for once cracking into some emotion as the Roller rolls on to Doris Day…

BREDA. Bitch!

CLARA. Gobshite!

BREDA. Shut it!

CLARA. A cup of tea a cup of tea a cup of tea!

BREDA. We can't have tea!

CLARA. Where's me tea!?

BREDA. She won't give us any tea.

CLARA. ME CAKE, ME CAKE!!

BREDA (*covering her ears*). We can't have the cake!

CLARA. Me on her lap and I mix the flour with the eggs and the sugar and the coffee…

BREDA. I MADE THE BLOODY CAKE!!

CLARA. And I'm half-listening to the radio and her leg sends me up and down like I'm on a horse trotting.

BREDA *walks fast towards the coffee cake.*

Not galloping now! Never a gallop. She never does anything to harm me, what with me being her favourite! I want my cake, I want my cake…

BREDA *picks up the coffee cake and violently flings it towards* CLARA. *It smashes and disintegrates on the floor.*

*A pause as they both look down on it.*

CLARA *lets out a scream of complete anguish.*

*Enter* PATSY *fast with more fish.*

PATSY. All right, the ladies?

CLARA (*screams*). GET OUT!

*In an act of defiance* PATSY *throws the tray of fish on the ground.*

PATSY. Despite my best efforts to stay away I'm back with this tide. No rhyme, no reason, no purpose. As always the bleak welcome…

*He goes to leave.*

BREDA. Stay.

*PATSY turns back.*

Close the door.

PATSY. You want me to step inside? Like a visitor?

BREDA. Do it.

*PATSY closes the door.*

*A long pause.* PATSY *can hardly believe he's finally inside.*

CLARA, *sobbing over the cake, mumbles a 'Hail Mary' to herself.*

Speak to me about your romantic loves.

PATSY. There's nothing to speak of. It's not that I hadn't wished it but in a town this size we've all got our roles to play and mine is to play a man of no great purpose… Might I sit down…

BREDA. Don't be getting ahead of yourself!

PATSY. Yes, Breda.

*A slight pause as* BREDA *stares at a very self-conscious* PATSY.

BREDA. Off with your clothes.

*A slight pause.*

PATSY. My clothes?

BREDA. Isn't it like me you are?! Now off with your clothes, Patsy.

PATSY. I don't feel that way about you, Breda….

BREDA. Do it! Clara… Water!

PATSY (*to himself*). Jesus.

> PATSY *nervously starts taking off his clothes.* CLARA *fills a basin of water.*

BREDA. What chance the baby, Patsy? Only born and spat out into dirt. Little baby lying in the cot listening to the words clogging the air. Stepping outside and finding his feet and the poor baby marked by even more words. What chance to keep him clean when the poor creature's turned grubby from the amount of words filling the space, filling your head. Stamped by story, aren't we, Patsy?! So what chance any man or woman against the idle word? The idle word?! Sure, there's no such thing as the idle word. Branded, marked and scarred by talk. Boxed by words, Patsy. Those bitches in the cannery and the gossip rising above the machines. All talk of Clara and Breda and The New Electric and the Roller Royle and the broken hearts. Mocking talk all week turning the streets narrower around us. Them nasty words crashing about from Monday to Friday and locking that front door behind us. What chance for the broken-hearted and the fishmonger to keep clean when people have the making of us? No mystery, no surprise…

CLARA. …no chance.

BREDA. Marked from early on. What words do you hear branding you, Patsy? 'Lonesome', surely? And 'lumpen' and 'ugly' and 'lonely' and 'foolish' and 'fishy', surely. Surely 'fishy'. Here he is, the 'fishy' fishmonger. And how you might pass and hear all those other words, at once, chasing you, Patsy. Chasing you through the little streets. Well, no more, hey! Isn't it time for a rewrite?

PATSY (*excited*). It's well time, Breda! Well time!

PATSY *stands in his shabby underpants in the basin of water with* CLARA *ready to scrub him clean.*

BREDA. Scrub away then and reborn, Clara!

CLARA *starts vigorously scrubbing him.*

Off with them words and all those stories pasted together and stuck on your back. Wipe away all them lazy images that others pin on us, Patsy. Get clean of that awful smell of fish and guts while you're at it. Strip away letter by letter and them terrible words will surely fall, won't they?! Fall back to the rot where they belong.

CLARA (*struggling with the smell*). Christ!

BREDA. Right out of the hospital and the little baby boy all powdered fresh and standing right here in front us, by Christ! Cleaner than clean with not a single word in earshot against him. No words to name and brand. Like you were spat out of your mother and found yourself standing in your underpants right here in our front room all these years later.

CLARA *continues for a while and then stops scrubbing him.*

CLARA (*catching her breath*). He's done.

PATSY (*smells his skin*). Jesus, like baby skin.

BREDA. And start then.

BREDA *hands the Roller Royle's suit to* CLARA *who starts to dress* PATSY *in it.*

…With the good news spread like wildfire. Standing out into town and the world is claimed as his in an instant. Caught unawares and the world's taken by 'the one and only' as he walks about town and everything moves to his pulse. The cars being pumped along the cobblestones, the little to and fro of people popping in and out of their houses, the shifting patterns of light on the water, even the tides themselves… everything moving for him, from him. The whole world his Faithful. The women who'd gladly go all the way and the young men aping the great man himself.

PATSY. Such pants.

BREDA. Sure, what woman could remain upright with this man about? Some heartless, bloodless, idiot dyke but no other woman, surely? And people's great weapon of words at first seduced and silenced, overawed and struck dumb. At first this silence, but then slowly from a whisper it grows. Oh, it grows, Clara, can't you hear it?

CLARA. Oh, I can, Breda, I can!

BREDA. It starts in a quiet breath and takes to the air, Patsy. A little breeze gets a hold of it and moves it about the house and towards the door and outside. Outside then and a breeze along the cobblestones takes it and through the little sewn-up streets it moves. It moves from breath to breath and the breeze stronger and it stronger too and it's taken to the harbour where the bigger wind takes a hold of it. And passed from breath to breath over the bay and sea and shared out amongst the airstreams it takes to the world and is taken in every breath in every word to everyone. Do you know what it is?

PATSY. Not a clue, Breda.

BREDA. 'Adoration.' Adoration for one man.

CLARA. That suit looks lovely on ya, Patsy.

*The new* PATSY *transformed in the Roller's suit.*

PATSY (*overawed*). Jesus, Mary and Joseph.

BREDA. Sit down at the table and a new day for us then.

PATSY *sits.*

ADA *walks out from her bedroom and sees* PATSY *sitting at the table. She stops. He immediately stands.*

I thought it time for a visitor.

*A pause.* PATSY *feeling very self-conscious as* ADA *just stares at him in the suit. She then goes to the table and sits opposite him.*

BREDA *puts a plate of two plain biscuits in front of them.*

*He's a little taken aback with the pathetic lunch but* PATSY *begins to eat it nevertheless.* ADA *picks up her biscuit and starts to eat it too.*

*A very long pause.*

PATSY. No chance of a cup of tea? It's a little dry.

*There's no answer. He continues to eat the biscuit.*

ADA. What is it you have to say to me, Patsy? Something new maybe?

PATSY. Something... new? (*Slight pause.*) Yes.

*Deep breath and nervously* PATSY *stands up and settles himself. He then speaks.*

The, emmm... the little cobblestones...

BREDA. Louder, Patsy.

*He resumes.*

PATSY. The... little cobblestones and they take me to the harbour. I meet you by the harbour, Ada. You're there in your good clothes and me in this terrific suit. And we talk about the fish in the seas and whether the fish have any notion of what awaits them on the land. Christ, if they only knew the torture that awaited them, surely they wouldn't be swimming in packs...

CLARA. New, Patsy! New!

PATSY. So, ahhhh... So, anyway... we're walking through the town and up through the little streets and we can hear the gossip from inside the houses, so you hold my hand then...

BREDA (*prompting him*). And your beautiful face.

PATSY. What?

BREDA. Say it!

PATSY (*fast*). ...and then Bernie Doyle, she's there... and we're having a conversation about Nana Cotter's one-hundredth birthday party and the great selection of sandwiches that were on display...

BREDA. And your beautiful face!

PATSY. And Mr Simmons limps over and we're talking about his new hip.

Apparently it doesn't need any lubrication which is news to me as I was always under the impression…

BREDA. Patsy!

CLARA (*covers her ears and barks*). Fish yes yes. No yes fish.

PATSY (*panicking*). …We're walking up the hill now, Ada, and the climb of the hill is lesser to us. Past the cannery and into Sheila and Robert's house and Robert's putting on his dancing-instruction video and going through the moves with real precision and dedication, fair play to him…

ADA *stands and turns away from him.*

…and I'm no longer sitting in the corner just watching but I'm centre stage with the lovely you now, Ada. Me and the lovely Ada and we're dancing with the pictures of all these exotic islands around us and Robert sipping on a soda water and saying what a great match me and Ada are. 'You're a great match, you two!'… He says…

ADA *goes towards the front door.*

…And afterwards and we're all having a game of Scrabble which I win with the word 'haddock'… a triple-word winner…

ADA *opens the door and* PATSY *thankfully stops talking.*

*A long pause as* ADA *looks out on the outside and the three others look at her.*

CLARA. There's a lull. Sort of lull that can get you worried. Pass me the bowl, Breda, it's time!

ADA. You can leave now, Patsy.

PATSY. Romance doesn't come too easy for a fishmonger, Ada. You can see I tried…

ADA. You leave, I stay, that's the order of things here.

PATSY. But maybe a song…

BREDA. Leave, she said.

PATSY. Music can say it better than these awful words, surely!

PATSY *frantically putting a cassette into the tape recorder.*

BREDA. Go, Patsy! Away from the door, Ada!

PATSY. Just one more chance! Fuck it, one more go! Something
to fan the flames of love! The music's playing, so the lights
to set the scene, Ada, please! Please! Please!

PATSY *stands on the table, ready to sing his song.*

*The opening chords to 'Wondrous Place' begins.*

*The door remains open.* ADA *turns off the light inside.*
PATSY *lit only by the light streaming through the open door.*

PATSY *sings for* ADA. *He begins nervously.*

> I found a place full of charms,
> A magic world in my baby's arms.
> Her soft embrace like satin and lace –
> Wondrous place.
>
> What a spot in a storm,
> To cuddle up and stay nice and warm.
> Away from harm in my baby's arms –
> Wondrous place.
>
> Man, I'm nowhere
> When I'm anywhere else,
> But I don't care,
> Everything's right when she holds me tight.
>
> Her tender hands on my face,
> I'm in heaven in her embrace.
> I wanna stay and never go away –
> Wondrous place.
>
> *Instrumental.*
>
> Man, I'm nowhere
> When I'm anywhere else,

> But I don't care,
> Everything's right when she holds me tight.

> Her tender hands on my face,
> I'm in heaven in her embrace.
> I wanna stay and never go away –
> Wondrous place.

PATSY *performs wonderfully. It finishes with the air charged with something new.* BREDA *switches the light back on.* PATSY *a little self-conscious.*

A song my poor dead mother taught me.

BREDA (*very hesitant*). Was she pretty, your mother?

PATSY (*staring at* ADA). Like Doris Day, they said. And him a decent singer, though I never learnt of his name or met him even. Last thing I had to do with him was my conception in the car park...

ADA. Of The New Electric Ballroom.

*A slight pause.*

PATSY. Yeah.

BREDA *remains standing and slowly pisses herself. A small pool forms around her feet.* ADA *looks at this happening and then back to* PATSY.

ADA. Doesn't story always find a way to catch us out, Patsy?

PATSY (*innocently*). It does. Story's a funny fish, all right.

*A pause.*

ADA (*a little confused*). What a difference you are to me suddenly. (*Pause.*) Time to start anew, you and me?

PATSY. Yes please, Ada.

ADA *stares directly into* PATSY*'s eyes. A pause.*

ADA (*softly*). The town still asleep I cycle to the cannery as always. I sit in my office with the machines crashing inside and tinning the fish. I look over my accounts and turn fish into numbers. I cycle home and the town quiet as always. I see people but talk to no one. A day like any other day. (*Pause. Somewhat nervous.*) But a different day... because of you. Everything coloured by you, every movement, each second passed is touched by you. The town sewn up by you. Tone and air changed knowing that you are close to me. It's me and you, you and me. (*Pause.*) And then it starts as a quiet whisper 'tween two little old ladies who watch us pass by. And it takes to the air. A little breeze gets a hold of it and moves it along the cobblestones and through the sewn-up streets it moves. It moves from breath to breath and the breeze stronger and it stronger too and it's taken to the harbour where the bigger wind takes a hold of it. And passed from breath to breath over the bay and sea and shared out amongst the airstreams it takes to the world and is taken in every breath in every word to everyone. (*Pause.*) The world knows of our new love. It's love.

PATSY. It's love. (*Pause.*) I'm standing in the little shoebox I call my bedroom, Ada.

I'm standing in my underpants and I'm staring down on my little bed. The pillows dented from where we lay our heads. The shape of us marked out on the bed, mapping out our night's sleep. The house quiet as always. The little stairs groaning as always. Everything as always but for this warm feeling in my belly. You're sat in the kitchen waiting there, Ada. And you touch my face. We're at the edge of things now and about to leave behind the safety of all we've known before. So turn to the door and open a life of possibility...

ADA. And enter then...

PATSY. And enter then...

ADA. And enter then...

PATSY. And enter then...

ADA. And enter then...

PATSY. And enter the outside and the cobblestones and sewn-up streets and salty air and the possibility for further away.

The outside and destinations unknown and my world blown
right open by 'chance', by this chance to change. And in an
instant I'm part of the living, the free, the 'fateless', the
unmarked and I can see me joining those seagulls and taking
my pick of life, and led by airstream and breeze, my life
made open by your hand in mine. Your hand is in mine and
showing me the open road of possibility, a horizon of chance
and what then? Like being taken to the harbour and just a
little drop we are. And taken by the tides and out further by
waves and currents and further and further still until our little
town is a sad memory, a bad joke.

My life a sudden adventure with my hand in yours. So what
details then? What details, Patsy!? Suddenly I'm drunk on
possibility! We're sheltering from the rain and you kiss me.
I'm curled against your back listening to your snores. I'm
sat on the bed and smiling at you singing in the bath. I'm
holding you in my arms with you twitching between sleep
and wake. I'm watching you laugh at something stupid I
said. We're stood in a crowd and you're touching my back.
We're dancing in Sheila and Robert's with our faces
together. We're sitting in Bingo and filling in the same
sheet. We're stood at the harbour and watching the horizon
and we take to the sea then and the waves take us and the
world opens to us further and further and I'm holding your
hand. Your hand holding my hope. Your hand holding my
hope. Your hand. (*Pause*.) Christ! Already something's got a
hold of me. In one breath all love is good and it keeps me
and this love it fills me… but with each step taken and a
different love, a fragile love, a love blind, surely. I let go of
your hand and walk away fast. And I want for the lover's
walk and the lie-ins and the kisses and the sweet
remembered details, the slow romance and the sudden lust
of love, but my heart tells me that the risk is far too great.
It's too great, Ada! We're walking hand in hand but you're
not really there. We're sitting side by side but you are
somewhere else maybe. I'm curled against your back but
your back's colder to me somehow. I'm kissing you with a
kiss that lasts seconds too less for me but seconds too more
for you. It's not you, it's not you! And what words do you
pin to me? 'Lonesome', surely. And 'lumpen' and 'ugly' and

'lonely' and 'fishy', surely. Surely 'fishy'. A man whose
only companion is fish and now sewn together with another
heart?! Fuck it! My own heart's too scarred by days and
nights alone. Too set in its ways by years of chit-chat to
little old ladies. Too scared to face into the unknown with
just love as a map! I'm stood still but already travelling the
lonely road and with each yard travelled it's more distance
between me and any wish for what it is to be in love, this
reckless love! And the wind is on my back and the seagulls
above mocking me! The narrow streets of our town they're
narrower. The houses on either side leaning in that bit close.
They're squeezing me, hurrying me away from any
possibility of a different life! My heart's ripped out and the
ground underneath is loose with the cliffs receding. I see the
harbour being sucked into the sand and the cliffs pull back
like you would pull a curtain back. And now this great space
with me running over it towards nothing, towards no home,
towards no place, Patsy. My heart ripped out and I can't
stop running! I can't stop!

*A long pause.* ADA, *frozen in shock, is looking towards*
PATSY *for some explanation for what she's just heard.*
PATSY *can't look at her.* BREDA *and* CLARA *look at* ADA
*and await her response. Suddenly* ADA *gasps for air. For
the very first time her eyes have filled with tears.* PATSY
*turns and leaves fast for the outside. The front door slams
shut by itself behind him.*

BREDA *presses the tape recorder and a new story is told.*

BREDA. It's time and looking in the mirror and this feeling of
everything not too right.

Stood in the bedroom and your forty-year-old body tries to
shake off these doubts.

Staring back a woman who's never been kissed.

CLARA. And it was only yesterday…

BREDA. And it was only yesterday and happy with the pattern
of things. When routine woke you with the familiar… the
pattern safe, life given a purpose. And what now all of a
sudden…?

CLARA *begins to dress* ADA *in the rara skirt and red blouse*.

'Cause still staring back, a woman who's never been kissed. So outside and take to the streets and cycle to the cannery and the machines, to those distant voices and bad words that locked the door. And inside, inside then. And the stories take over and our pattern returns.

CLARA. The lovely pattern of things.

BREDA. By their nature people are talkers. You can't deny that. You could but you'd be affirming what you're trying to argue against and what would the point of that be?

BREDA *aggressively swipes* ADA*'s face with lipstick*.

Just adding to the sea of words that already exist out there in your effort to say that people are not talkers. But people talk.

CLARA. Fish fish fish. Yes no fish! No yes fish!

*A very long time where* BREDA, CLARA *and* ADA *are silent*.

ADA, *costumed ridiculously, face covered in lipstick, stands with tears streaming down her face*. CLARA *sits and stares down on the remains of the sponge cake*.

BREDA *stands still and silent, holding and listening to the tape recorder as the sounds continue for a while. She turns it off*.

*Then*.

Will we have a cup of tea and some of that nice cake you made, Breda?

BREDA. Yes, Clara.

*A pause*.

ADA. Will I make the tea, Breda?

BREDA. That would be nice.

ADA *goes to the kettle and turns it on and watches it boil*.

*It boils.*

*Blackout.*

*Silence.*

*The End.*

# PENELOPE

*Penelope* was first performed by Druid Theatre Company in Druid Lane Theatre at the Galway Arts Festival on 13 July 2010. The production subsequently toured to Edinburgh, Helsinki and New York. The cast was as follows:

FITZ                     Niall Buggy
DUNNE                    Denis Conway
BURNS                    Tadhg Murphy
QUINN                    Karl Shiels
PENELOPE                 Olga Wehrly

*Director*               Mikel Murfi
*Designer*               Sabine Dargent
*Lighting Designer*      Paul Keogan
*Sound Designer*         Gregory Clarke

The play received its London premiere at Hampstead Theatre in February 2011, with Aaron Monaghan playing the role of Burns.

**Characters**

BURNS, *mid-thirties*

QUINN, *mid-forties*

DUNNE, *about fifty*

FITZ, *mid-sixties*

*…and* PENELOPE, *twenties*

*After a little time we realise that we're looking at a dilapidated swimming pool drained of water. There are two ladders at the back of the pool where the actors enter.*

*At the back and above the swimming pool we can see a large sliding glass door that leads into a villa. There's a scrim which allows us to see inside, when appropriate.*

*The pool's been turned into a living space and it seems to have operated as such for years.*

*There are five battered pool loungers of different makes and sizes (some inflatable), a miniature snooker table, a trestle table stacked with beer, wine, spirits and snacks. There's a portable CD stereo. There's also a large helium-filled heart-shaped balloon bobbing above the table. Under the table there's a mass of junk.*

*There's a standing screen, at the back in the corner, large enough for someone to change behind it unseen.*

*There's a large gleaming Taunton Deluxe Barbecue raised on a wooden pallet in the very centre of the pool.*

*Most importantly there's a CCTV camera in the pool looking down at the men.*

*When the lights come up we have time to take all this in as the two men on stage are very still. We could be looking at a picture.*

*One of the men is standing beside one of the ladders holding a sponge full of pink suds. He's been cleaning a long streak of blood off the tiled wall by the ladder and stands there staring at the drips coming down the wall.*

*This is* BURNS.

*A man in his mid-thirties, he wears a short Terrycloth swimming-pool robe, scruffy trainers and battered spectacles. He looks strong and able but carries himself subserviently.*

*The other man is standing looking intensely at the Taunton Deluxe Barbecue.*

*This is* QUINN.

*He's a powerfully built, mid-forties man. His dyed black hair perfectly set, he's immediately a man of some vanity. He's wearing tight red Speedos and a pair of smart brown moccasins.*

*The stillness is broken when* QUINN *quickly walks to the barbecue.* BURNS *turns to look at him.*

QUINN *reaches out his hand and holds it above the grill to test its temperature. As usual it's cold. There's an uncooked sausage on the grill. He picks it up and looks at it. He drops it back down.*

*He walks quickly back to the trestle table, stops and throws a look at* BURNS.

BURNS *hesitates. He was about to say something but decides not to.* QUINN *wants to hear it.*

QUINN. What do you have to say? (*Slight pause.*) What is it?

*A pause.* BURNS *gathers the courage.*

BURNS. I need to talk about Murray.

QUINN *puts on the stereo and Herb Alpert and the Tijuana Brass play 'Spanish Flea'.*

QUINN *finds a blowtorch amongst the snacks. He turns back and looks at the defunct barbecue like he means business. The blowtorch fires in his hand. He walks back over to the barbecue and begins blasting the sausage. He's cooking it for breakfast.*

BURNS *drops the sponge into his metal bucket. He can't get rid of the last of the blood on the wall. He returns the bucket to under the trestle table. He starts to look for something on top of the table. He finds it and puts it on. It's a cardboard cone-shaped party hat that elasticates under his chin.*

*At the same time two other men appear and climb down the two ladders at the back. They're also dressed in Terrycloth swimming-pool robes.*

*As they turn to us we see* DUNNE.

*A man of about fifty. He carries himself like an old theatrical troubadour (in flip-flops). He goes straight to the table to fix himself a cocktail, ignoring* BURNS *completely. He dances a little to the music for his own entertainment. He can move.*

*The other man is* FITZ.

*A trim and fidgety mid-sixties man. He carefully organises his pool lounger and towel. Everything has to be in its place. He's brought an old book to read and takes real care that his bookmark is doing its job. He has a small container of tablets. He empties the contents out. There's only three tablets in there. That will do. He throws them into his mouth and knocks back a bottle of tomato juice. He blesses himself. That was the wrong direction. He tries it again and again but has forgotten how to bless himself. He gives up. His manner's a little fey.*

DUNNE *meanwhile has fixed his cocktail. It's a very flamboyant margarita topped with fruit and tiny paper umbrellas. He walks over to watch* QUINN *pulverising the sausage.*

BURNS *remains at the table where he's placed various snacks into various bowls. He acts as a reluctant servant throughout.*

FITZ *acknowledges him with a little nod.* FITZ *turns and looks at the blood on the wall.* BURNS *does the same.*

*The two men then look over at* QUINN.

QUINN *turns off the blowtorch and hands it to* DUNNE.

*He reaches into the barbecue and grabs the sausage but burns his hand.*

QUINN. Shit!

BURNS *doesn't have to be asked. He comes to the barbecue, grabs the ferociously hot sausage and starts to blow on it for* QUINN.

*A perfect temperature now and* QUINN *finally takes the sausage in his hand as 'Spanish Flea' comes to an end.*

*The men speak with considerable erudition. They may be of different classes (*QUINN *is certainly a rougher diamond) but they all like the sound of their own voice. Their accents are provincial (each one from a different area of the country) though sound soft… as these are men of distinction.*

QUINN *bites into the sausage.*

DUNNE. How is it?

*A pause as* QUINN *carefully chooses his word.*

QUINN. 'Sausagey.'

DUNNE. That's good.

FITZ (*to* DUNNE). Most are often not. Some are. Some have got a sausageness but more often than not they taste of nothing but heat.

DUNNE. And heat isn't even a taste.

FITZ. Isn't it?

DUNNE. People would say that heat was a sensation, you know… generally…

QUINN. As a rule.

DUNNE. As you say, Quinn… as a rule… the word having its meanings… having its related characteristics, Fitz. 'What does heat have?' 'Taste' is not the first thing that springs to mind.

QUINN. 'This tastes hot.' I would say that before I would say this tastes of sausage.

DUNNE. But I said, 'How is it?' and you said, 'Sausagey.' Why didn't you say that it tastes hot if hot was your first sensation?

QUINN. Hot was my first sensation but I said 'sausagey' out of badness.

DUNNE. Right.

QUINN. This is the very last sausage, men, and I wanted you all to know that it's a superior sausage. Not some dust-filled, cigar-shaped, hunk of pigshit… but an actual sausage! The sausage of our youth. Had I just said, 'This is a hot sausage'… well, that has negative connotations…

FITZ. Not if we were cold, it doesn't. A hot sausage would be quite nice in the cold!

QUINN. Obviously not if we were cold, Fitz. Had we been sitting in a yurt in Mongolia shivering into a herd of yaks and I was clutching this sausage… I would look you each in the eye and smile… 'Gentlemen, this is a hot sausage! The last hot sausage! The final sausage, heated! What do you feel about that then, lads?'

FITZ. Jealous. And cold.

DUNNE. Leaning in trying to get a modicum of heat off that delicious-looking banger, no doubt.

QUINN. But this is not Mongolia…

FITZ *and* DUNNE. God, no…!

QUINN.…this is… Burns!

BURNS. What?

QUINN. What is this?

BURNS. A sausage?

QUINN. Yes, it's a sausage! What are we here?

BURNS. 11.30 a.m.

QUINN. More importantly!

BURNS. Thirty-three degrees Celsius.

FITZ. That's hot.

DUNNE. That's hot and early.

BURNS. It's always hot.

DUNNE. And invariably early…! (*Trails off.*) when it isn't late…

QUINN. And this… my fellow competitors… this is sausagey.

QUINN *starts to eat the sausage as the others look at him.*

The early bird, men… early bird…

QUINN *begins to nibble at the sausage, impersonating an early bird until it disappears into his mouth. He swallows.*

Done.

QUINN *opens his mouth to show that it is gone.* DUNNE *inspects it.*

DUNNE. Even after all this time, the competition.

QUINN. What else is there?

DUNNE. You're right.

QUINN. There's nothing else!

DUNNE. I need to be reminded of that on a daily basis so as to maintain my edge!

QUINN. You do.

DUNNE. I didn't have to do that as a younger man, we all remember that! My body still holds a physical memory of the attack of my youth but the mind wavers. It's a waverer!

FITZ. The mind is the enemy!

DUNNE. The mind is a bucket of eels, lads! It obviously is with us four, given our emmm… What would you call it?

QUINN. Situation.

DUNNE. Given our remarkable situation. I am an afternoon away from turning to jelly… so it's important to remember that the fight is still on, lads!

QUINN. It most certainly is.

DUNNE. Good!

QUINN *glances over at* BURNS *who stares at the blood on the back wall.* DUNNE *shows a coin to* QUINN. *He waves his other hand over it and it disappears.*

QUINN. Seen it.

FITZ. Must say there's some days I'd welcome the degeneration. A life in jelly doesn't sound that bad. I'd miss reading of course. Conversation you can keep. Words are cheap, Dunne...

DUNNE. Cheap and nasty.

FITZ. ...but reading... the classics in particular... the companionship of Homer...

DUNNE. I never read a book in my adult life.

FITZ. That surprises me!

QUINN. Nor me.

FITZ. Well, that's less surprising really...

QUINN *didn't like that insult*.

DUNNE. There was only ever one book I cared for as a boy.

FITZ. And what was that?

DUNNE. *The Magic Porridge Pot*.

QUINN. That's the only book there is.

FITZ. There are others actually.

QUINN. Not that speak so clearly of investment and growth or the fast development of an unstable economy.

DUNNE. Oh, right?

QUINN. This is a whole town that ground to a standstill when it became awash with porridge, yeah...

DUNNE. Interesting.

QUINN. ...a pot that gave and gave, a community that took with no notion of responsibility or future.

FITZ. I thought the magic porridge pot lifted the people out of poverty.

DUNNE. And into obesity, those fat bastards!

QUINN. Can you imagine eating yourself through porridge 'cause you can't get out of first gear? Or imagine the consistency of a heart fed on a diet of sweet stodgy oats. Jaysus!

FITZ. Crikey.

QUINN. What the pot needed was regulation. It needed that little girl to stay at home with the sole purpose of saying, 'Cook-pot-cook' and 'Stop-pot-stop'. Outside of that she didn't need any more words.

FITZ. She would have grown up retarded, mind you.

QUINN. She would have grown up in power.

DUNNE. She'd be the keeper of the pot.

QUINN. Exactly! She'd be the keeper of the pot.

DUNNE. Fascinating read!

QUINN. Lovely pictures!

FITZ. Which is the reason why I'd miss reading! It's that type of mental stimulation, that access to ideas and colour and character! Without this book, without this unequivocal bond between me and it… (*He kisses his book*.) I imagine a hellish jelly! Absolutely hellish! And yet for all of that there's still a lot of pluses to senility as it's such a huge effort to maintain the fight, isn't that right, boys?

DUNNE. You forget the prize.

FITZ. You do forget the prize. You, Burns? Do you forget?

BURNS. Do I forget what?

QUINN. The prize!

BURNS. No.

DUNNE. I can't either.

QUINN. Nor me.

FITZ. Or me! I wish I could. I lie to myself that I can but of course I can't. I'll tease myself with the notion of senility, distract myself with Homer but really, truthfully… of course I can't forget the prize.

DUNNE *grabs a hold of his stomach and moves it slowly. The others watch.*

*He stops and picks his drink back up.*

DUNNE. It's impossible to say exactly what physical shape I would have morphed into had my journey sent me elsewhere. What a fascinating thing the body is, gents.

FITZ. Remarkable, really.

DUNNE. And your body, Fitz? Tell me and tell me with honesty now… do you lament the obvious muscle wastage, your kindling-like bone structure, the fact that your skin resembles a shrunken piece of yellowing parchment?

FITZ. Somewhere on life's journey the body goes its separate way. My head reconciled a few years ago that I was no longer 'the man that I was', Dunne.

DUNNE. Very wise.

FITZ. Something your head must have done in its youth, what with your…?

DUNNE. With my…?

FITZ. With your considerable…

DUNNE. My considerable what…?!

FITZ. Your considerable geography…

DUNNE. [*'I understand you.'*] I have you.

QUINN. The day the head and body part company is a tragic day for the self. I am what I was in my early twenties, exactly the same, lads… like some sensuous ninja. Beyond that! Improved upon! Controlled. You treat the body with respect and in return it will repay the head a thousand per cent.

DUNNE. Percentages aside, Quinn, I will always allow my body to take the lead over the wavering head. This is the man I am!

QUINN. All stomach, you mean.

DUNNE. It's the gut that's led my life, that powers my performances here in this pool.

QUINN. Gotcha.

DUNNE. Of course I'd be a more svelte animal had I had a more emm… a more ahh…?

FITZ. A more productive existence?

DUNNE. As you say… but the body must be respected for what the body wishes and the head must support the body, not unlike the lowly oxpecker bird who must feed on the back of the obscenely large hippopotamus. The body, boys… the body is always the king.

QUINN. Or kingdom.

DUNNE. Or kingdom, yes, Quinn. Depending on one's…

BURNS. Appetite. Depending on one's appetite the body is one's king or kingdom.

DUNNE *fires* BURNS *a look. He's spoken out of turn. Slight pause.*

DUNNE. A dictum you may put to use one day, my boy. Looking a little peaky this morning.

BURNS. 'Peaky'?

DUNNE. Like a bulimic buck after a long day's frolicking.

BURNS. Okay.

DUNNE. Like an emaciated kidney after a long day's filtering.

BURNS. Understood.

DUNNE. Get a sandwich into you. Where's the Twiglets?

BURNS. The table.

DUNNE. Fetch 'em then!

BURNS *hesitates. Not to go would make things worse.*

DUNNE, *for some reason, does a fantastical flamenco step.*

BURNS *goes and fetches the bowl of Twiglets for* DUNNE. *He returns with the bowl and hands it to* DUNNE.

Divert your eyes, ya scamp!

BURNS *doesn't. It's quite a moment.* FITZ *and* QUINN *turn and look.*

BURNS *and* DUNNE *stare into each other's eyes. If anything,* BURNS *is being the more aggressive.* DUNNE *picks up a Twiglet and quickly turns away from* BURNS *with the bowl.*

FITZ *returns to Homer and is immediately engrossed in the book.*

FITZ (*whispers to himself about a certain piece of text*). Very very good.

QUINN *walks to the back wall and looks at the bloodstain on the tiles. He begins to do some press-ups against the wall, his face centimetres from the blood.*

BURNS *watches him until he can't any longer.*

*Out of frustration,* BURNS *suddenly slaps his own face. SCHLAP! They all look at him.*

BURNS. What?

FITZ (*noticing* BURNS*'s party hat*). Is it the weekend already?

DUNNE. Well, the hat's on, so it must be.

FITZ. Where does time go, hey, Burns!?

BURNS. Turns into cancer apparently.

DUNNE. Only seems like yesterday that it was yesterday.

BURNS. It was yesterday.

DUNNE. I was right then. Right again!

BURNS. Right.

QUINN. Time's a tragedy, men.

FITZ. Hey, my mammy used to say that! That exact phrase, 'Time's a tragedy.'

QUINN (*sarcastic*). Well, fancy that! So did my mother!

FITZ. We might have had the same mother, Quinn!

QUINN. We could have done, I suppose.

FITZ. Of course we would have met in childhood, right?

QUINN. Not necessarily, I never mixed with my family.

FITZ. Oh, that's an interesting psychological fact!

QUINN. It was a joke.

FITZ (*laughing*). Oh, very good! Very clever.

DUNNE (*laughing*). A very funny joke, Quinn. Very funny humour!

QUINN (*cold*). Right.

FITZ. Well, she was never a woman for words, my mother. She could talk but I was always of the opinion that she hated the debris that conversation left behind. She couldn't see the point of offering an opinion on anything!

QUINN. Your mother was a woman, right?

FITZ. Oh, completely! And rather than thinking of her as a halfwit, I like to think of her as a revolutionary! Had her ideas on vocal abstinence caught on, you could imagine, boys, a world with absolutely no wars. Or had there been wars they would be enacted through mime…

QUINN *mixes a cocktail like a professional.*

…a quiet, sparse, thoughtful world devoid of the yap yap but unfortunately populated with the leotard and the whitened face of the mime artiste.

DUNNE. A wonderful illusion, mime!

DUNNE *begins performing some mime as the others look on. He plays a man trapped in a box.*

QUINN. Every empire has its price to pay, Mr Fitz.

FITZ. Yes, that's very true.

QUINN *opens an invisible door on the invisible box.*

QUINN. Get out.

DUNNE *steps out.*

FITZ. Was your mother brilliant in any way, Dunne?

DUNNE. 'Brilliant', no. God, no! She left little imprint on the world, my mother, except for her size. She was a fat lady and unpleasant with it. I was still wetting my bed as a teenager and I put that down to a total absence of physical affection. I found the only way to get a hug off her was to season my neck with a little gravy.

FITZ. Mothers and sons, will we ever escape their influence!

DUNNE (*grandly*). Books will be written! Plays will be expelled... and the great mystery of mother and son will continue to baffle like the mystery of yeast!

QUINN. What are we going to do about this fucking barbecue?

FITZ *and* DUNNE *walk over to* QUINN, *and the three men look at the barbecue like it was a spaceship.*

*Finally...*

BURNS. You could kill it.

QUINN *turns and looks at* BURNS.

QUINN. It still holds promise. Still has hope for us.

DUNNE. What does man have but 'hope', Burns.

BURNS. Fuel would help.

FITZ. It did fire that very first time... when was that?

QUINN. A few years back.

FITZ. As long ago as that!?

DUNNE. Remember how it came, all wrapped up and addressed to us, in our names?

FITZ. Oh yes, that was a great day!

QUINN. It was, yeah.

FITZ. I miss that day.

DUNNE. The box was in the middle just here... or perhaps there... and we had no idea how it got down, remember. A crane. God's hand. A team of magical fairies dedicated to outdoor cooking. It was mysterious and extraordinary, wasn't it, lads?! And so we awoke from our *fata Morgana* and stood perusing the box and discussing in detail its removal. In time we agreed on a procedure and then we carefully lifted the box upwards to reveal this stunning barbecue... not unlike the historic moment Howard Carter unsealed the doorway into Tutankhamun's burial chamber. Wonderful. (*Slight pause.*) And then we put Burns in the box for a little bit.

BURNS. For a day.

DUNNE. A day!?

QUINN (*smiling*). It was a day and a night.

BURNS. You taped the box back up and left me in there for twenty-four hours.

FITZ. That was a little cruel. Are you sure?

BURNS. Yes, I'm sure.

FITZ. And why did we do that, I wonder?

DUNNE *and* QUINN *are laughing.*

BURNS. Boredom probably, I don't know, I couldn't hear the conversation. I was concealed in a mountain of foam peanuts like a plastic toy in a Kellogg's box.

DUNNE (*losing it*). Holy God!

QUINN. We were excited though, right?!

DUNNE. Beyond excitement!

QUINN. We let you out in the morning and apologised.

DUNNE. And you accepted our apology.

BURNS. That's right, I did.

FITZ. Well, that's good! (*Praising* BURNS.) And gracious.

DUNNE. But it was a mystery, wasn't it?

FITZ. It was.

DUNNE. The sender unknown, and me and Fitz and Murray sat about speculating the sender's identity while Quinn fired up the barbecue. Oh, we had big dreams then! Massive! I'd imagined us standing around like a group of friends, eating hot meats, drinking cool beers, talking business into the early hours.

QUINN. But it farted out a tiny fire and has since been extinguished. Bastard.

DUNNE. It's a garden tragedy, is what it is! A real bastard!

FITZ. We should have removed it a long time ago. It's actually mocking us by sitting here! It's placing unworkable images in our heads, boys. It's a pornography!

DUNNE. I hate that fucking barbecue!

FITZ. Might we get rid of it, Quinn? Please!

QUINN. We'd never get it up the ladder.

DUNNE. Have we ever tried?

BURNS. You made me try once.

DUNNE. And what was the outcome?

BURNS. A slipped disc.

QUINN. I had a dream about it last night. Dreamt that it was on fire.

*A long pause. The other three are immediately in shock.* QUINN *turns and sees this.*

(*Carefully.*) What is it?

DUNNE. I dreamt that too.

QUINN *on edge now.*

FITZ. And me too, Quinn.

*The stage is charged with fear.* QUINN*,* FITZ *and* DUNNE *look at* BURNS.

QUINN. And you?

BURNS. What?!

QUINN. You had a dream last night. Did you see the barbecue on fire?

FITZ. You know what it means if you have…?!

DUNNE. Just say it if you have!

QUINN. Did you have the dream or not, Burns!

BURNS. Yes! (*Slight pause*.) At the start of my dream it was on fire.

*A pause. They are all shook, terrified.*

FITZ. So tell the dream.

*A pause.*

QUINN. The fire starts underneath the barbecue. It starts at the same time he steps from his boat onto the shore and looks up at the house here. The fire fills the barbecue's frame as his feet take to the sharp rocks. He glances over at our white houses huddled together by the cove, creaking and empty. He could crumble them with a breath but he couldn't be bothered, he wants us and our blood. He knows what we've turned his house into, how we spend our days here in his pool. How Penelope sits in that room watching us… doubting that he's alive maybe… and maybe choosing one of us for love. This is our hope, our religion… but today her husband returns. (*Slight pause*.) The barbecue he must have sent it to taunt us… it burns and he's here. (*Slight pause*.) He's running up the pathway, the cypress and hyacinth heavy in the middle of the day, they fill his head and wipe out in an instant his years of exile, of war, of the journey home to her… the longing for Penelope. He's over the parched grass now and smelling the poisonous barbecue snaking up into the air and he can hear us in the pool. She's standing there with happy tears in her eyes but he doesn't go to her but to us and to his knife. And if only it were quick but he's in amongst us ripping apart our legs and we're scurrying about the floor like whingeing bloodied slugs. He pulls Fitz aside and makes us watch. He fillets him. And

how easy the blade cuts him up. He shatters his old bones with
his hands. He moves… hacking up limbs and tossing innards
aside like he's looking for something in Fitz. Flesh is landing
on the grill, the barbecue mocking us this final time. And Fitz
is falling in and out of consciousness but he's slapping him
awake, he's spitting beer in his face, he wants to see his eyes,
have Fitz see what he sees. He cracks open Fitz's chest,
reaches in and takes his heart in his hand. (*Slight pause*.) And
their eyes lock together now… and he squeezes his heart
slowly. Ever so slowly. (*Pause*.) He's looking at one of us
three. He's smiling. And we're next.

*A pause.*

Is that how we all saw it?

FITZ *and* DUNNE *nod.*

QUINN *looks at* BURNS.

BURNS. Yes.

QUINN. Right. Then it will be today.

DUNNE (*barely audible*). My God.

*A pause.*

FITZ. I never thought I'd have the backbone for suicide but
faced now with the likelihood of watching my own backbone
being removed and flung onto that barbecue, I think it's only
fair that I should give suicide a shot.

DUNNE. A shot we can't do… we have knives though.

FITZ (*panicking*). Why didn't these knives feature in our dream
as weapons of defence?!

DUNNE. Courage, Fitz, courage!

FITZ. I'm pretty handy with a knife! I whittled a penny whistle
out of some beechwood once. Beechwood as we all know is
a very hard wood and the blasted thing took me the best part
of my summer holidays to carve. When I went to play it… it
whistled like a dying breath. Exactly the same noise… and a
similar stench. But knives I can do, Quinn!

BURNS. I don't want to die in that pain! Not by him, not here, not today!

QUINN. And you won't die!

BURNS. There's nothing we can do, Quinn!

DUNNE. We arm ourselves, is what we do!

QUINN. We do not arm ourselves! We know the man we're dealing with here! This man is a colossus! This is a man who went to war and butchered thousands without breaking sweat.

BURNS (*retching*). Oh God…

QUINN. A bowel movement sends us into palpitations! This is a legend who faced monsters, who remained unblinking, unfazed before he humiliated them into submission. Dunne has a phobia for autumn.

DUNNE. You say 'a phobia', I call it 'a legitimate fear'!

QUINN. It's a season!

DUNNE. It's a decaying, withering slow walk into the darkness of winter, is what it is!

QUINN. Stop it now!

DUNNE. Death I can do but the journey towards death, the long walk… The thievery of autumn when we are robbed of summer sunshine and led further into the depression of a dying year…

BURNS. Fuck it, I need a drink!

QUINN (*to* BURNS). Behave yourself now! Don't you dare drink!

BURNS *goes to table and hits the spirits fast*.

FITZ (*to* DUNNE). I never thought of autumn like that! You spoke there with the clarity of a great poet. I always had you pigeon-holed as a Master Derivative but now I see that actually I have neither a pigeon or a hole. For the rest of our days you are indescribable to me, Dunne.

DUNNE. Thank you.

FITZ. Of course there's a certainty that we're talking minutes rather than days…

DUNNE. Quite.

FITZ. And yet in those minutes you will be a laureate of our times!

DUNNE. My mother would be proud… had she not been a fat heartless bitch.

FITZ. Fix me a very large G and T, Dunne!

DUNNE. It would be my pleasure. (*Calls*.) Burns, fix him a sup!

BURNS. If we leave, we leave to nowhere! This island is miniscule! We hide in our houses and he'd sniff us out. We could row but we've already sold our boats for beer.

DUNNE (*outraged*). And not gin?!

BURNS. We could fashion together a vessel using our recliners… only to perish on the reef. None of us can swim!

FITZ. The irony being is that we've spent the worst part of our lives in a swimming pool!

BURNS. We are fucked and no amount of comedy is going to lessen that fact, Fitz!

FITZ. I am using levity, young man, as a tonic to see us through the next few moments before Quinn delivers to us a plan of action!

*They're all hitting the alcohol to calm down.*

DUNNE. Remember it was Fitz that he will fillet first. It will be Fitz that he will prepare for the barbecue!

FITZ. That's right!

DUNNE. And yet is Fitz wading through the doldrums of his subconscious?! Is it Fitz who is wandering aimlessly through the forest of disenchantment… sailing a sea of desolation… No, it is not Burns because Fitz is an Optimist…!

BURNS. A Cockeyed Optimist.

FITZ. I may very well be a little cockeyed...

DUNNE. In a certain light...

FITZ. In a certain light certainly... But I am happy!

DUNNE. You're also a little high.

BURNS. You're medicated.

FITZ. Yes. Extremely medicated.

BURNS. Do you have any more?

FITZ. Sadly only three pills entered my decaying belly. 'The Father, the Son and the Holy Ghost.'

BURNS. FUCK!

FITZ. Indeed. Quinn?

QUINN. We stay.

> QUINN *turns to them*.

> We do as we always do. Everything will change if Penelope agrees to take one of us as her husband today. If she does... he's left bobbing about the ocean like flotsam. The dream will have come to us and not to her. So it is a day like any other day. We sell our love to her as we do always but today with the support of the others. It is in our interest that someone at least wins her... so we work together, men.

BURNS. 'Together'? Us?! Oh, what shit...! SHIT SHIT!

QUINN (*to* BURNS). Enough!

> BURNS *gulps down the spirits and shovels in the snacks*.

FITZ. You're joking! The sort of men we are, Quinn! This is a joke, right?!

QUINN (*grabbing* FITZ*'s head like a hypnotist*). Gather all that you are, Fitz. Gather it, gather it!

FITZ. Right.

QUINN. Take every instinct, every impulse, everything you believe yourself to be and stand for. Take it, digest it!

FITZ. Done.

QUINN. Now shit it out! From this moment on we build anew, lads!

FITZ. A new what? What are we building?!

DUNNE. A company!

FITZ. An actual company!?

DUNNE. It is a company, right?

QUINN. Exactly…

DUNNE. A group of men with a common ideology, a collective direction! That's what you're suggesting, Quinn! We're building a company right here!

FITZ. Do we get to wear a uniform?

QUINN. We don't have time for that.

DUNNE. A motto! A motto's essential! Possibly in Latin.

BURNS. '*Is Res Non Vos Es Caro In A Assus.*'

FITZ. Meaning?

BURNS. 'It Matters Not, We Are Meat On A Barbecue.'

QUINN *slaps* BURNS *across the head with a table-tennis bat.*

FITZ. But how can I be certain that we are together? Could I really trust Dunne, for example?

DUNNE. The old Dunne – no.

FITZ. No.

DUNNE. No one could trust the old Dunne. I myself have had issues of trust with my very self – the old Dunne who has buried his morality beneath this festering pool. But the new Dunne that stands before you like a veritable Apostle of Goodness…

BURNS. In flip-flops.

DUNNE. In flip-flops, correct... I am at one with you, Mr Fitz. You can go beyond trusting me. You can erase the meaning of 'trust' in your heavily fingered dictionary and supplant it with my very own face.

FITZ (*backing away*). Jeepers.

QUINN. Embrace it, Fitz!

FITZ (*it's new to his mouth*). Embrace 'trust'??

DUNNE (*holding out his arms*). Embrace 'trust'!

> QUINN *and* FITZ *talk to each other as* DUNNE *slowly approaches, arms outstretched.*

QUINN. Though every fibre of your being – (*Pointing at* DUNNE.) recoils at even the sight of this man...

FITZ. Yes...

QUINN. Although you probably heave as I too heave at Dunne's efforts of seduction... Today in front of Penelope we stand beside Dunne!

DUNNE. Embrace me, Fitz!

QUINN. His success is our life...

FITZ. Oh God...

DUNNE. Support, respect and unite around me, men!

FITZ. It won't be easy.

QUINN. It will be very difficult.

FITZ. Especially with Dunne.

QUINN. It will be agony.

DUNNE. But how men build and how we survive! Sure, aren't we wired for change. If not we'd still be communing with those hairy apes.

BURNS. Some of us have no choice!

QUINN. Some of us are more comfortable in the company of monkeys… subservient-bespectacled-little shitheads! But not us three! Not now!

FITZ *embraces* DUNNE.

FITZ. We are company!

QUINN (*chuffed*). We are company, Mr Fitz!

BURNS*'s head drops.*

DUNNE. We are one voice! Now gather! GATHER!

QUINN *points up to the CCTV camera. It's pivoting and looking down at them.*

QUINN. You're playing for our lives, Dunne! Seduce well… and may the gods spare us!

*The red light goes on on the camera and a follow spot beams down on* DUNNE.

*The beautiful* PENELOPE *can immediately be seen through the scrim, sitting in a seat and watching a large television and the live transmission inside the villa.*

DUNNE*'s on. He steps up to a microphone and looks to the camera.*

*In seduction,* DUNNE *is even more outlandishly theatrical.*

DUNNE. You wake! And down the hill across the cove, through my little blue door, into my Crackerbread house… I too awake, Penel… ope. Somehow your first morning's breath rides the treacherous wind and finds its way to my own nose and awakens me! (*He smells.*) And it is a fine breath! Not the claggy-acid-breath of a stomach made stagnant by a night's sleep… the type of breath that could peel a hard-boiled egg… oh fuck, no! But a breath that perfumers would battle to bottle. A breath bursting with pheromones! Is it any wonder it builds a mighty tower in my underpants. A tower that I take to the shower and lather with peasant olive soap…!

QUINN (*exasperated*). Jesus Christ…!

DUNNE. The shower falls upon me like…? like butterfly kisses and I think of you in your chamber, beneath your shower, madame.

QUINN. And what lucky drops they are…

DUNNE. Oh yes! When one thinks of the useless life of some water. The dark days of toilet water, for example. Water used for nothing more than filling a cistern and pulverising a petrous turd…

QUINN *grabs him, pulls him out of his light and whispers…*

QUINN. Focus on her!!

DUNNE. It's all for her! I'm channelling this poetry through her…! I will not be edited by a lesser scribe!

QUINN. You reason with him, Fitz!

DUNNE. Reason with creation?! I will not be reasoned with!

QUINN. You are not an actor!

DUNNE. Unhand me, sir!

FITZ (*snaps*). For God's sake, Burns, do something!

BURNS *turns to them and raises his bottle.*

BURNS. I am. (*Slight pause.*) I'm escaping.

BURNS *drinks.* FITZ *has an idea. He places a new CD in the stereo. 'Morning Mood' from* Peer Gynt *begins.*

FITZ (*to* QUINN). Can't do any harm.

DUNNE *resumes his attempted courtship, the pastoral music embellishing his already turgid lyricism.*

DUNNE *drops his robe. He's wearing tiger-print Speedos.*

DUNNE. I'm standing, Penelope, on my roughened tiled floor, drying my naked body in God's morning sunshine, the Ionian breeze drying the tear-like droplets from my bristling shoulders.

FITZ. Oh, that's nice, Dunne. Very nice.

DUNNE. A bird? A bird makes me turn to the open window… a blackbird on my sill and what a dainty little fellow with his singing… warming what cockles are left in my arid heart.

QUINN. The more he sings, the more he speaks of you, Penelope.

DUNNE. Is it a message then, Quinn?

QUINN. A message, yes.

DUNNE. A what…?

FITZ. It is a call, Dunne!!

DUNNE. Yes, a siren, I would say, Fitz! For all at once I am under that bird's spell. The singing, it creates a carousel in my mind! It churns within me, rebuilding me, refashioning me, reupholstering an even greater Dunne, more Godly Dunne, more Well-Done Dunne!

QUINN. You step outside with that bird flying above you leading you to her beauty, her grace, Penelope's arms.

DUNNE. Oh yes!

QUINN. The sharp rocks conspire to see you imprisoned in your lonesome cove, that tiny house…

DUNNE. Bastards!

QUINN. …but you, Dunne, you are a new man! Fashioned by the power of her love!

FITZ. And how the cypress and hyacinth greet him, Quinn.

QUINN. Today like no other day, for they see the man he has become, Fitz.

FITZ (*impressed by* QUINN*'s poetry*). Nice.

QUINN. They see the transformation love can have… on even the most… (*He can't help himself.*) annoying of fuckers.

DUNNE. And yet… dear fellow travellers… I have mortal doubts. (*Slight pause.*) How can I even be in Penelope's shadow? How can I taunt myself with the idea of a touch… not so much a touch but even a kind look? She is beyond words, beyond description. Even a master scribe as I am can not conjure up her beauty in tiny letters, in exhausted words.

QUINN *wants to thump him*.

I walk over the parched grass, the lavender alive with a million bees all looking at my new self but sensing my familiar nerves. Their buzzing adds within me layers of doubts... doubts upon doubts and how these doubts round my shoulders and wrinkle my brow and buckle my knees... (*He collapses on the ground*.) till I am bent over on all fours like a wounded hound, wishing away his life, longing to be put asleep eternally, placed in a bucket and pushed out to the calm of the Ionian Sea. (*Slight pause. Whispered*.) I am... nothing to her.

DUNNE *whimpers and sobs a little*.

QUINN *and* FITZ *share a look. They should leave the old ham on the ground but they need to recharge him*.

QUINN. And yet... she calls you.

*A pause*.

DUNNE (*feigning weakness*). Calls me? Does she, Quinn?

QUINN. The bird again sings... and this time by Penelope's open door. The melody of the bird's voice, of what it means, has you standing again, Dunne. Anxiety falls from your fingertips... and evaporates.

DUNNE. What power I feel.

QUINN (*instructing him*). Well, get up then.

DUNNE *gets his body upright*.

DUNNE. Blood surges through my powerful body, it puffs colour into my cheeks, thickens my hair, fattens my arms, boys! (*Like some primal roar*.) YOU WANT ME! (*Slight pause*.) Each step towards the open door and I stand on shards of your husband's past, Penelope! I crush beneath me his heroics! I claim them as mine!

QUINN. All right, Dunne...

DUNNE. I move quickly through the door! Into your home and your memories of him, Penelope! (*Losing it.*) I take those memories and devour them… (*He devours them.*) and in an instant I am your memories! I am claiming this house for the years of longing… of waiting… for the 'what ifs' and 'maybes'. Do you not recognise my past!?

QUINN. Stop it…!

DUNNE. The man I was, the respect the world showed to me! Do you not see in me… PEDIGREE?!

*The red light on the CCTV goes off,* PENELOPE *disappears and the camera pivots away from* DUNNE.

*This infuriates* DUNNE *even more. He turns from the microphone, runs to the ladder and begins to climb it.*

I have given my life to a possibility of love with you…! But you have turned me into this… this notion of a man who BEGS!

FITZ *holds on to* DUNNE*'s legs as he tries to get out of the pool.*

I am worthy of this house, of this prize, but you have reduced me, Penelope… to a fat man in SPEEDOS, FOR FUCK'S SAKE!

DUNNE *collapses on the ladder.*

*'Morning Mood' continues gently to its end. It seems even more foolish now.*

DUNNE *quietly steps back into the pool and* FITZ *helps him back on with his robe.*

BURNS *wanders over to him and hands him his margarita as 'Morning Mood' comes to its natural end.*

BURNS (*whispers to* DUNNE). Love… your… work.

*Furious,* QUINN *takes* BURNS *firmly by the arm and leads him away from the other two to have a word. They stop and stand facing each other.*

QUINN *suddenly smashes him across the face.*

QUINN. What are you doing?

BURNS. Expressing my dissatisfaction!

QUINN. About what?

BURNS. THIS, QUINN!

QUINN. Get me a drink, Fitz!

BURNS. Oh, I couldn't get Murray's blood off the wall, by the way!

QUINN. Right.

BURNS. You'd think on a tiled surface it'd be easy. Remarkably tricky… and then there's the grouting…!

QUINN. You're not going to help us then?

BURNS. There's no point. We're the talking dead. Now I want to talk about my friend Murray…

QUINN. Go on then…

BURNS. And what happened…

QUINN. Wasn't really a surprise, was it?

BURNS. He was all I had here…

QUINN. You were in love with Murray?

BURNS. I loved him as a friend…

QUINN. You're joking me!

BURNS. It's possible for a platonic love to exist between two men… even in a drained swimming pool, even after all this time living in each other's stink…!

QUINN. Well, if you say it's possible, it might very well be.

BURNS. We were close…!

QUINN. I never saw it.

BURNS. It was the beginning of a friendship!

QUINN. And to be cut short so tragically! My God!

BURNS. You killed him…

QUINN. I thought he slit his own wrists! Didn't he slit his own wrists, Fitz?

FITZ. Like a professional!

BURNS. You spoke him into a corner, scraped away any possibilities he may have had! We all saw you doing it and did nothing to stop it! He was my friend, Quinn…!

QUINN. He was competition! Jesus Christ! A 'friend'?! (*Slight pause*.) I sat around listening to him talking to Penelope and the words he could use and how he would bring those words together. I'd go home to that shitty little house by the cove. I'd go over my new courtship, re-edit, redefine, restructure. All this time I can feel Murray itching away, yeah. Always the better sale than me, always the clearer presentation! He was the best of us, right?

BURNS. She seemed to like him best.

QUINN. Right, so I got into his head, of course I did!

BURNS. I saw.

QUINN. I got close and Murray makes the mistake that we're friends suddenly. And I see little insecurities in him and we're speaking the same things… that we're all living this hell and the gods have forgotten us and that there is no Penelope even… there's only us in our little houses, us making the journey up the little path to this empty house, us in the pool trying to think of new ways to win a love that's un-fucking-winnable! 'She's not even there, Murray!', I say. 'The gods are not up there any more! We are being eaten by madness!' I'm speaking at him so that he has no time to speak himself. I wear Murray down like an old rag! He's not Murray to me any more, he's not even human. We share little pleasantries in the morning but I'm steering his moods, counting his words, building little corners and placing that little fucker in those corners! I might have just slit his throat but where's the sophistication in that, Burns? That's common! You understand that, right?! We've got a lot of time on our hands down here! We are all here to win and each second is a game! So let's play the game! We are all men of business! We bring what we were in the old world to this place! We are all the same type of men! Murray would sell his dead granny for a deal. He would have to find her grave first, 'cause let's face it, he wouldn't have showed at the funeral. He would buy a spade, go to that grave, dig her up, crash her out of that coffin, throw her in the back of his Lexus and sell her decaying, filthy arse because he loved money! We are all like that, Burns!

BURNS. I don't want to be like that any more…

QUINN. You feel some allegiance to me, Fitz and Dunne?

BURNS. To a point, yes…

QUINN. Great! Then you won't have any problems getting onside and helping one of us win Penelope! Now shut the fuck up, get off the drink and get onside! (*Turning to the others*.) So it's me up next, men! The Mighty Quinn! What happened, Dunne… oh Jesus, man…!?

DUNNE. Obviously the day that's in it, Quinn…

QUINN. Right.

DUNNE. Went for something traditional, something that may appeal to her more literary sensibilities but I couldn't control my bile.

QUINN. I find a shit in the morning helps.

DUNNE. I hope I live to see my next movement.

QUINN. And me mine.

DUNNE. Whatever the outcome, whether it's my murderous death or losing Penelope to one of you three, they were my final words of romance, sadly.

QUINN. That is a tragedy.

DUNNE. Had I made it into her house and arms I feel certain that I would have investigated a life in theatre. I have a musicality and subtlety all of my own. How and what I performed just ten minutes ago is a complete mystery to me.

QUINN. It's the mark of a great artist that you found truth in such wonderful delusion.

DUNNE. Thank you, Quinn. That is a consolation.

BURNS *walks back to the back wall. He traces his finger down the bloodstained grouting.*

QUINN. You look a bit tight, Mr Fitz!

FITZ (*trying to read his book*). Feeling a bit tight, Mr Quinn… just trying to stave off images of my barbecued flesh and lose myself in the companionship of some epic poetry.

QUINN. You stay in that happy place, Fitzy!

FITZ. Understood.

QUINN. I've been working on a new pursuit that may very well be my greatest illusion yet! With Dunne having shot his load and Murray dead I'm clearly our best bet today, right, men?

FITZ. Yes, definitely, Quinn.

DUNNE. Absolutely.

QUINN. Burns has got all the passion of a corpse and, with drink taken, is about as useful as a cock in a convent… you, Fitz, let's be honest…

FITZ. Please do.

QUINN. Your seduction has all the skill of a fingerless fool filleting a fish.

FITZ. That's true.

BURNS *quickly goes to the table, grabs the metal bucket from underneath…*

QUINN. What you have in me, gentlemen, is consistency! Prepare yourself for the moment consistency meets innovation…!

BURNS *flings the metal bucket against the wall. Bloody water splatters everywhere.*

*A pause.* BURNS *calmly walks over to* QUINN. *He stops beside him.*

BURNS. Can I just step into your shit and have a quiet word?

QUINN. Say it now, I'm about to change.

*A pause.*

BURNS. I am no longer your junior, Quinn. We are all equals as of the moment we had our prophesy.

QUINN. Well, if it makes you happy to think that… fine.

BURNS *takes off his party hat and flings it aside.*

BURNS. Let me say it clearly so you understand the direction of the day and the day's probable outcome.

QUINN. Make it quick.

BURNS. For the short remainder of our lives… you will continue to use your notions of love to entrap this desperate woman. The more you talk, the more you steal the world of any truth. Today I can finally see that clearer than ever. (*Slight pause.*) I have no hopes now but for this one hope, Quinn.

QUINN. Yeah and what's that then, lover?

BURNS. That after squeezing the life out of Fitz's heart… her husband turns to you… bends you over… reaches up your arsehole and rips out your poisonous brain. I want to live to see that.

BURNS *raises his bottle of spirits and makes a toast.*

Let real love speak!

BURNS *drinks.*

*Suddenly the red light appears on the camera, the follow spot beams down on* FITZ *and* PENELOPE *is seen watching her television.*

FITZ *is 'on'.*

FITZ. Oh, crap….

DUNNE (*loud whisper*). Quinn!?

QUINN *turns and sees* FITZ *is 'on'.*

QUINN. Oh, for FUCK'S SAKE!

FITZ *places his book down on his pool lounger, walks to the microphone, stares up at the camera and begins very badly.*

FITZ (*terrified*). Now that I'm… is it not…? the… how can I in words…? there are… they say at least… as I would… unconditionally… speaking…

QUINN *and* DUNNE *go to the trestle table and fix themselves some drinks as* FITZ *crumbles in front of them.*

…and often should be… listen with an open… Penelope. Am I not…? I concur with previous… with an honest… setting aside all… between elements of… (*Pleads.*) Quinn, please help me!

QUINN *turns and looks at him but offers him nothing. He walks behind the standing screen in the corner.*

Dunne?

DUNNE *turns away from him.*

FITZ *knows he's alone. He tries to drag up anything from his drug-addled mind.*

And if I could… and if it was possible I would. (*Slight pause.*) Because back inside here… (*Slight pause.*) back in the place where no one can see… (*Slight pause.*) there's little pauses, little pools of nothing. (*Slight pause.*) And I can be there. Deeper than the deepest sleep with no thoughts, no itchy wants throwing me into the next thing, the next page, the next piece of noise. I can be there. (*Slight pause.*) And maybe I can stretch this nothing further and is it possible to take these pools of nothing and shape a new world? Is there anyone who can stop me other than me? So I go about constructing a house out of this material, place this nothing house on a nothing island, by a nothing cove, in a nothing atmosphere. Place my glorious nothing self in this nothing house and bask in nothing. In the real world people are shunted from scene to scene, packed with half-knowledge, half-truths. What a world they've made! And where does truth exist and how does anyone breathe in that world? How do doors open and how do people leave their houses? And what makes them want to talk or need to listen or feel obliged to experience things? And how is it possible that they can fall asleep and rise again and fill a day and mark that day and sleep and wake and live in that world? It's called living apparently. How horrible that world is! But I'm in my house of nothing and high in the distance I can see those people on Earth 'living'. I look at them indifferently, without conscience, without pity, it means nothing to me because I am a world onto myself now. Here alone, a body, a house, an atmosphere, wonderfully indifferent, blissfully uncaring. My body pumps and breathes independently and I've ordered my thoughts so that now I have few thoughts or perhaps I've no thoughts any more. When I think of my youth and what I have sold and what I have gathered and what I have lost and what I have gained and what little effect my youth has had on any existence! I am a blemish, Penelope! A tampering twit who's used life, tossed it aside, rolled it in my fingertips, placed it in an ashtray, pushed it down the back of the couch, flicked life across a tabletop! But I will forget my past, forget the real world, sit in my nothingness and begin with a new idea... an idea... of... (*He clears his head and the word forms.*) you.

FITZ *takes a breath.*

PENELOPE *is seen standing up from her seat. From behind the curtain she looks towards the pool.*

BURNS *and* DUNNE *don't see this as* QUINN *remains behind the screen, changing.*

I put aside all the stories I've ever made about you, all the dreams I've ever dreamt, of which there are millions... what use are they when they are nothing of you. But still I must begin somewhere with some idea of you. And I do. (*Slight pause.*) The idea arrives not as a physical thing or a smell or a scent of any sort but this tiny feeling. And it begins in my stomach because it's stomach-felt and it bleeds into my heart and it holds the heartbeat.

PENELOPE *raises the curtain and looks down on* FITZ. *For the first time we see her true beauty. She hasn't aged. She is a woman in her early twenties.*

And it grows in an unchartered place this feeling but in a world of nothing it is the only thing I have and I help it grow inside me and I allow it to claim my small world, my whole self. It takes everything that I am, that I want to be and it will lead me to you in time.

QUINN *appears dressed in a black morning suit. He's staring at* PENELOPE *and the connection* FITZ *has made with her. He's panicked.*

And lead me through the tedious detail of the island that I have spoken and dreamt into extinction. Lead me to opening my door, to taking a chance. I long for love! For this all-consuming love as you must long for it. And in truth it is nothing of you, the physical you but it is everything that this feeling is! Do you understand this?!

QUINN *is looking for something. He finds* FITZ*'s beloved book and walks over to the barbecue. He places it on the grill.* FITZ *doesn't yet see this as he's hypnotised by* PENELOPE.

How it holds my heart and how I know after all these years of longing for your husband it must hold yours too…! Can you see in me a possibility? A possibility to keep love faceless… and just love the love itself!?

QUINN *walks back to the trestle table, grabs the blowtorch, fires it up and walks back to the barbecue.*

We are two souls longing for a love to grow from a glorious nothing! Throw open your door and let us start with care…!

QUINN *pulverises Homer.* FITZ *suddenly sees what he's doing, breaks and races to the barbecue.*

MY GOD, NO! NOOOOOOOO!

*He pushes* QUINN *aside and rescues his book.* FITZ *falls to his knees and frantically puts out the flames.*

*The curtain drops on* PENELOPE, *the camera switches off and she disappears.*

QUINN *turns off the blowtorch and walks back to the trestle table and puts the blowtorch back.*

BURNS *suddenly spits a mouthful of whiskey into* QUINN's *face.* QUINN *grabs at his eyes as* BURNS *punches him in the head.*

*The two begin to fight badly.*

DUNNE *walks up to a sobbing* FITZ *as he tries to put the book back together.*

DUNNE (*to* FITZ). Just the one note?

FITZ. What is it?

DUNNE. More energy. And don't be afraid of the gag.

*A slight pause.*

FITZ. That's two notes.

DUNNE. Second one was free.

BURNS, *sitting on* QUINN's *chest, screams in anger/frustration.*

*He's holding a Peperami above his head like he's going to stab* QUINN.

QUINN. Is that a Peperami in your hand?

BURNS. Probably. Maybe. Is it? (*He looks.*) Yes.

BURNS *holds it to* QUINN's *throat.*

QUINN. So what do you plan to do?

BURNS. I don't know yet.

QUINN. It won't kill me if that's what you have in mind.

BURNS. I'm compiling a list of possible ways to murder you, force-feeding you reconstituted meats I'll happily add to that list.

QUINN. That will take a lot of patience.

BURNS. I have a lot of patience.

QUINN. Patience you might have but Peperami and time you don't. He's coming!

BURNS *gets off him.*

He's coming, men! He's coming!

BURNS. All this time she's never opened her curtain and shown herself but it was Fitz's words and for the first time honest words…!

FITZ. And it's impossible to say where this honesty has come from!

DUNNE (*grandly*). From the tiniest light within your darkened soul.

FITZ (*in awe*). Holy God!

DUNNE. Of course she may have been stunned by my poetry earlier…

QUINN (*to* DUNNE). Oh, shut up!

BURNS. We had a chance, Quinn!

DUNNE. …woke from her reverie and searched out my melodious tones! She did meet my eye just then, Fitz! Fleetingly it was but we stared into each other's hearts at that very moment. In hers I saw devotion and can you guess what she saw in mine?

FITZ. Stenosis.

DUNNE. Yes, obviously… but seeping from my thick ventricles she saw… 'honour'.

BURNS. Has honour ever lived here, Dunne?

DUNNE. What are you talking about!? We are men of integrity, Burns! I shit honour!

BURNS. But will you ever return to reality?

DUNNE. What reality?

BURNS. *A* reality!

DUNNE. I am in one!

BURNS. A reality closer to what the people of the world may ACTUALLY RECOGNISE! I mean, look at us!

DUNNE. How dare you bring the world into this! I have spent a lifetime escaping the world! What the fuck has the world ever given to me?!

FITZ. Given you nothing but you've taken enough!

DUNNE. I most certainly did! And I am owed Penelope's love!

BURNS. But your words have meant nothing to her! She's an object to you, an ending, another deal! Look how she reacted to Fitz just now. He was speaking not to trick her and win his way into her house but he spoke with a simple truth from his heart!

FITZ. Faced by my immediate barbecuing I have developed a goodness! Holy shit!

QUINN. It had nothing to do with your words! Her husband is close, her heart can feel it... now more than any other time she is open to seduction!

FITZ. But it might have been with me, Quinn!

QUINN. And how could I live with myself knowing that you'd be in that house?!

BURNS. But we would have been saved from a terrible death!

QUINN. And beaten by him! Alive but knowing that she was stolen from me! This is Fitz we're talking about here! Look at him, for fuck's sake! No offence, Fitz...

FITZ. We're past that...

QUINN. ...but this is a decaying man, an incontinent near-imbecile, a man whose manhood has shrivelled to boyhood... could you happily deposit this geriatric at her door!? Of course you couldn't!

BURNS. So the fight continues.

QUINN. Of course the fight continues!

DUNNE. And we're opposition again?

BURNS. We always will be.

FITZ. This working together? This company!

QUINN. An aberration!

FITZ. This trust?

QUINN. A deviation!

FITZ. Excellent!

DUNNE. Then can I add that Fitz is also a junkie!

FITZ. I step into that madness with all the happy expectation of a plankton drifting the oceans of the world, Dunne. You are a jealous bastard!

DUNNE. And you are a terrible bastard!

FITZ. You have all the erudition of a pig defecating his day's feed!

DUNNE. Your brain has the consistency and the imagination of that pig defecation!

FITZ. Shithead!

DUNNE. You are the shithead, thou vicious mole of nature!

> DUNNE *flings a Twiglet into* FITZ*'s face.* FITZ *grabs a half-eaten sandwich and throws it at* DUNNE*'s face.* DUNNE *grabs his Martini and throws it in* FITZ*'s face.* FITZ *grabs his gin and tonic and throws it in* DUNNE*'s face.* DUNNE *slaps* FITZ *across the face.* FITZ *punches* DUNNE *in the stomach.*

> Enough! (*Drops to his knees.*) Enough!

BURNS. Not one of us is worthy of her, Quinn!

QUINN. I am worthy of her!

BURNS. Years ago as a healthier man you might have imagined it. But you saw her beauty just now! All these years and she is the same woman and even if she was seduced by your lies how could you even think of her taken in by your looks and that abomination you call hair!

FITZ. His hair's his best feature!

BURNS. His hair is fake!

FITZ. A wig?!

BURNS. It's dyed!

FITZ. A dyed wig?

BURNS. Just dyed.

FITZ. My God, really?!

DUNNE. No man is worthy of Penelope's affection when he wears his mock virility on his head! You fraudulent follicle-er!

BURNS. Stop talking like that!!

QUINN. What makes me worthy is that I'm stronger than you, Burns. Stronger than the lot of ya! I was born strong!

FITZ. Your melanin wasn't!

QUINN. I see that I'm losing her and straight away I'm thinking… I'll take death… whatever he carves me into… I'll take it over the humiliation of losing out to Fitz! That's how strong I am! Annihilation versus the shame…!

BURNS. So what have you won just now?

QUINN. Control, you idiot! You know that!

BURNS. How can you talk about love when you don't even have compassion for your own life? Me… I cared for someone!

QUINN. For Murray?

BURNS. It was the start of a bond!

QUINN. Did you feel some brotherhood with this man?

BURNS. Yes.

QUINN. Why?

BURNS. Why did I like him?

QUINN. Why did you feel you should like him?

BURNS. I wasn't consciously thinking, 'I should like this man…'

QUINN. Weren't you?

BURNS. He was my friend!

QUINN. What did you want from him?

BURNS. Nothing!

QUINN. Something.

BURNS. Companionship, trust…

QUINN. I know what you are and what men do… and what we don't do is 'trust'!

FITZ. It's true.

QUINN. You're sat opposite Murray and you're telling me you're not working out ways of beating this fucker!?

BURNS. I'm not!

QUINN. It's all just innocent chit-chat, little bits of banter that brings you and Murray closer together.

BURNS. It's called friendship, Quinn!

QUINN. You would smash Murray into the ground! What makes me worthy, Burns, is that I'll say it out straight! I will crush Murray, I will turn on each one of you because I must! You stand in my way and I'll chop you down because that is what I was, what I still am! How many men were here? At the beginning? How many, Fitz?

FITZ. A hundred or so.

QUINN. A hundred men living on this rock all fighting for her love, yeah. The weaker ones are out by that first summer. Years pass and more are driven mad, remember! We're queuing up to seduce Penelope but nothing happens and heads drop. Men are toppin' themselves every other night. Did ya care about any of those men?!

BURNS. No.

QUINN. Of course you didn't! You hated them like I did, right?!

BURNS. I hated some…

QUINN. And now you've all of a sudden got yourself some humanity?! Does it make you feel better that you can feel for another person? Makes you more whole, more human than me?

BURNS. Well, yes it does!

QUINN. You're a liar…

BURNS. I know what I'm feeling! The way we have lived… these shameless lives we've lived here…!

QUINN. We are the last men! We've survived here because we've understood our nature, Burns. Men go out into the world, begin a day with all notion of honesty, of law, of community. But you think that notion lasts!?

BURNS. If we tried to make it last…!

QUINN. What if our waking impulse is to feel at ease with life, yeah? Like life nurtures you and in return you give life back kindness, respect? That you allow life's annoying little mishaps, you take them on the chin, you meet badness with a little smile, a shrug of the shoulders. Some idiot's talking too loud or not making sense or plainly lying through his teeth but you allow his loudness, his idiocy, his conniving thieving ways because today, Burns, today you are in harmony with life! You are a virtuous man, a compassionate human being, a liberal hugger of humanity! For the brand new Burns, this is good, right?! This is how the gods would have planned it too. A planet of the merciful! Is that idea compelling to you, Burns?

BURNS. Yes!

QUINN. This new-found honesty that's suddenly lit up in your black… your blacker-than-black fucking soul, Burns… well, this new you must be banging his tambourine at this new world order, marching towards this glorious utopia…

FITZ. It does sound nice...

QUINN. It's a rainbow, is what it is, Fitz, and he knows it! We eat life! We annihilate every single thing that doesn't comply to our tastes, to our sense of good, our idea of beauty. Each second of the day is a challenge to control, to win, to shape, right, Burns?! Each little sight you see is there to be turned sour, yeah. Each person we meet is there to be beaten down and knocked into place. It's subtle at first, otherwise it's all a bit aggressive and a little too obvious for us men of the world. But idle chit-chat is there to be won, friendships are there to be used, love is a fucking weapon. This impulse, boys, this is what shapes life! This is our muscle! This is how we are the last four men standing! I'm working on reducing Murray, the great Murray, to some gibbering wreck, yeah! I'm wearing him down, placing that knife in his hand, placing that knife on his wrists and not one of you stepped in! Not you either, Burns! And why's that? 'Cause you wanted to see 'your friend' dead! I'm right, amn't I?!

BURNS. No...

QUINN. 'Cause you're one step closer to Penelope that way! In your stomach you have some tiny illusion to do good but every history of you, every fibre of Burns is carved from hate! Hate is our friend! Hate evolves our spirit, our dreams, our society! We came to this island to win the island and we'll use what we can to win her, to win our freedom, to win power! What do you know about love, Burns!? With whatever means you must triumph and crush... that is your one fucking belief! Without keeping that alive, what has your life been, man? Nothing!

*Silence as* BURNS, DUNNE *and* FITZ *stare at the all-powerful* QUINN.

QUINN *picks up the party hat and places it back on* BURNS*'s head.*

Now unless I'm mistaken... it's me up next, right? Same moves as before with some added illusion. Do you understand me?

BURNS *remains silent.* QUINN *goes for a softer approach.*

I won't be stopped. 'Less you toe the line I swear to God I'll cut you up like a crazed Boy Scout butchering a chicken. Can you imagine that?

BURNS. Yes.

QUINN. Good boy.

BURNS *stands hanging his head as* QUINN, FITZ *and* DUNNE *look at him.*

QUINN *gets the large helium-filled heart balloon and places it on the barbecue.*

His boat's close… I can feel it. He can see the island. (*Slight pause.*) Now get behind me, men.

QUINN *walks behind the standing screen.*

BURNS, DUNNE *and* FITZ *stand beaten. They're finished.*

FITZ *stares longingly into the empty tablet container. He turns it over and fails to shake anything out.*

FITZ. There's nothing to fight for. I always imagined my dying would be like this. I fought all my life and now I'm leaving with complete indifference. I have left… nothing.

BURNS. We're dead men.

*A long pause. Then…*

DUNNE. Gravity should at least take some of the blame. (*Pause.*) People can't help making things, nature decays and rebuilds in the blink of an eye… and the surface of the planet's so busy. These days it's difficult to remember where I've come from. I might close my eyes and shards of past lie next to bits of half-memories and it's impossible to tell whether I've featured in my life and what needs saving from it and what needs saving now. (*Slight pause.*) I turn off gravity and stand about and watch the oceans tumble into space, watch the animals and fish fall away from the Earth, see the little birds blown into nothing like dust. People cling to themselves and onto their machines and soon space is littered with centuries of debris. Up there and humanity doesn't amount to a great deal but down here on Earth it's

very quiet with just me lying on my back on the grass.
(*Slight pause*.) Lying in our garden somewhere between
awake and asleep with the sun on my face. I could easily fall
into sleep but the inside of the house is calling me. I stand up
and see my reflection in the kitchen window and I'm looking
at my ten-year-old self. I look down on my young hands and
walk my ten-year-old body towards the inside. Already in the
walk my heart feels lighter, the colours saturating around me.
There's no burden of the past here, no bad memories to taint,
no memories at all to colour, no future to ponder or tease…
just my ten-year-old self walking with the warm sun for
company and the expectation of a good thing. I enter the
house. And it's still inside the house. The temperature drops
a little and cools my brow. I walk to the kitchen and stop at
the door. (*Slight pause*.) I'm watching my mother taking a
glass from the shelf and filling it with milk. She opens the
press and takes out a packet of biscuits and places two on a
little saucer. I know it's my milk and biscuits. She feels me
watching her and turns around then. And I smile at her from
the door. The scene suspended then in its own space with no
past or future, no hidden story itching badly underneath, just
me with a smile on my mouth and the beginnings of a smile
in my mother's eyes. I let my heart lead me now and I move
and go to her and throw my arms about her. I bury my head
in that big chest of hers and she folds around me and kisses
the top of my head. Her breathing me up, me breathing her in
and both wanting to disappear into what…? into our love.
(*Slight pause*.) Gravity has done away with people and their
things and me and mother begin a new life. From our little
kitchen this love breathes out into the world. (*Slight pause*.)
And what happiness.

*This quiet revolution in* DUNNE *has stirred* FITZ *and*
BURNS.

*Suddenly the door into* PENELOPE'*s house opens. She steps
down and looks down at the three men.*

*She walks around the side of the pool, stops and stands just
above the CCTV camera looking at them. There's an
intensity to her. She's waiting. Something is going to
happen.*

FITZ (*aside*). We need to bury our corruption and let love survive this pool. Say it could be done, Burns.

BURNS (*aside*). We have been terrible men... and even now each of us knows what terrible thing must happen next. (*Slight pause.*) But I swear to whatever ounce of goodness I may still have inside me, boys... (*Slight pause.*) If we fight to let love win, even in death us three would be free.

DUNNE. Do it, so.

> BURNS *presses the stereo and 'Spanish Flea' by Herb Alpert and the Tijuana Brass blasts out.*

> BURNS, DUNNE *and* FITZ *look back at the screen.*

> *The French tricolour unravels over the standing screen as* QUINN *bursts 'onstage' costumed as a tiny Napoleon Bonaparte adorned with an oversized bicorn naval hat and naval uniform.* QUINN *immediately sees* PENELOPE. *This gives him immense confidence. He begins to play out a short scenario where 'Napoleon' slaughters imaginary enemies with his sword. He takes out a map and looks over the expanding French Empire. He turns it over and with a quill he mimes writing a love letter. He kisses it, folds it a few times and hands it to* BURNS. BURNS, *like the dutiful assistant, unravels it and magically it has turned into a paper dove.*

> QUINN *disappears momentarily behind the screen as* BURNS *'flies' the dove across the stage.*

> QUINN *reappears as a weeping Josephine de Beauharnais, wife of Napoleon. Only now do we realise we're watching a very accomplished quick-change cabaret routine with illusion.* QUINN *is dressed in a long silk dress, a brown wig curled around his powdered face. 'Josephine' sees the dove and tries to catch it but it is always out of reach. She pulls a pistol from her handbag and shoots it. The dove falls into her hands. Josephine opens the dove and reads the love letter from Napoleon. She breaks into a smile showing her rotting teeth and disappears behind the screen.*

> *'Spanish Flea' cuts into 'A Taste of Honey' by Herb Alpert and the Tijuana Brass.*

BURNS *holds out a walking cane for* QUINN *as he reappears dressed as Rhett Butler from* Gone with the Wind. *He takes the cane and swaggers about all Clark Gable-style, removing the French tricolour which suddenly becomes the American Confederate flag. In his hands the cane becomes a large bunch of flowers. He throws the flowers to* BURNS *who catches them.*

QUINN *disappears behind the screen once more.*

*He suddenly reappears as Scarlett O' Hara in bloomers, corset and bonnet. 'She' snaps the flowers out of* BURNS*'s hands and smells them. The flowers wither in her hands. She falls to her knees, cries and waves a fist at God for mercy.*

QUINN *goes back behind the screen and immediately appears above the screen as Shakespeare's Juliet at her balcony.*

*'A Taste of Honey' cuts into 'I'll Never Fall in Love Again' by Herb Alpert and the Tijuana Brass.*

*Another drape falls over the screen showing flowers on a garden trellis. A tiny sparrow lands on 'Juliet's' hand. Juliet pets it and suddenly it becomes a vial of poison. She throws it in the air and* BURNS *just about catches it.* QUINN *vanishes as* BURNS *places the vial on a tiny silk pillow.*

QUINN *reappears as the distressed Romeo. 'Romeo' sees the vial of poison, cries and lays his head down on the pillow. He drinks his own poison and 'dies'.* BURNS *places the standing screen drape over Romeo's body. From underneath, Juliet suddenly reappears, distraught. She takes Romeo's dagger and stabs herself. She 'dies'.*

BURNS *grabs* QUINN*'s feet and drags him back towards the screen.*

*He nods at* FITZ *and* DUNNE *to get ready to attack.*

*'I'll Never Fall in Love Again' cuts into 'America' by Herb Alpert and the Tijuana Brass.*

BURNS *and* QUINN *are back behind the screen.* FITZ *and* DUNNE *rifle through the debris on the table, looking for something to kill* QUINN *with. They find various useless implements and stab the air with a corkscrew, snooker cue, a tennis racket, etc. Finally* DUNNE *finds a knife.* FITZ *takes it off him.* FITZ *wants to do it. They face the screen.*

QUINN *reappears costumed as Jackie Kennedy with* BURNS *costumed as JFK. They wave from their car when suddenly 'JFK's' head explodes. 'Jackie' cradles the dead body like* La Pietà *and cries.*

QUINN *then stands and takes off his Jackie costume. Underneath he is dressed as Eros the Greek God of Love with wonderful wings.*

*'America' cuts into 'Zorba the Greek' by Herb Alpert and the Tijuana Brass.*

QUINN *takes the heart balloon, cuts its string and holds it out to* PENELOPE. *He lets go of it and it floats up and into* PENELOPE's *hands.*

PENELOPE *is about to smile.*

*Suddenly* FITZ *is over fast. He stabs* QUINN *on the side.*

QUINN *grabs at the wound and turns to* FITZ.

QUINN (*gasping*). You whittled a penny whistle…? You fucking liar!

DUNNE *grabs* QUINN *and holds his arms back.*

DUNNE (*shouts*). Finish him!

FITZ *stabs him again.* BURNS *is over fast, takes the knife and drives it into* QUINN's *stomach.*

BURNS *pulls the knife out and* QUINN *falls to the ground, the balloon exploding in* PENELOPE's *hands.*

PENELOPE *turns away fast to re-enter the house but…*

BURNS (*calls*). Wait!!

FITZ *slams off the stereo.* PENELOPE *stops but doesn't yet turn around.*

I'm trying to be good…

*Like* DUNNE *and* FITZ, BURNS *is covered in* QUINN's
*blood.*

PENELOPE *has remained still.* BURNS *needs to speak but
has drawn a blank.*

*A pause. Then quietly to start…*

Outside of here there must be a world. (*Slight pause.*)
There's other places and colours and there must be cities
and towns and villages with people, right? Stories must
clash about and finish abruptly or start afresh and live for
moments or maybe days even. And these stories must be
shapeless and free and twist into new directions and
possibilities. And the people who live these stories must
have frustrations and worries… they must be annoyed by
these stories and have anxieties about the outcome of these
stories or have excitement about the stories' possible
endings… I don't know. And people move about from one
story to the next, from a moment's conversation to a whole
life's dialogue, maybe. And outside they have this and
people can get to live in this shapeless incredible…
adventure. (*Slight pause.*) And it's not just words 'cause
mostly life outside is lived by just looking and being in the
world. And a corner is turned and a new world opens up and
you look down and about and marvel that men have shaped
homes from water and dust. Towns disappear into
countryside and then into sea and sea into new lands and
people get to live a life where possibility, where freedom is
brought to life by the simplicity of waking up and sitting up
in bed and just being in the world. Can you imagine that
life? (*Slight pause.*) But the brain wakes in the morning and
so drunk it is by digesting the world that it wants for order.
And what the brain wants the brain gets. Rules are placed on
stories, talk is a veil for lies and people carry around little
pedestals of differing sizes and half-talk to each other and
lie to themselves and others that they are part of a
community, part of a civilisation probably. But it needn't be
like that, Penelope! It shouldn't be that way! And what if
people could open their eyes and sit up in bed like the very
first time and just be in the world and let their hearts rule?
(*Slight pause.*) Today felt closest to that day. (*Slight pause.*)

I woke at the moment I wake every morning, stared at the ceiling I've stared at a thousand times, rolled over in bed and looked out on the Ionian Sea sitting there like some picture postcard. Already each second, each breath, each thing I see feels brand new. It's like my heart has been clicked on and the everyday is brighter suddenly. Things that have sat about lumpen, things that have imprisoned me in their dreariness and routine are now alive. And it's Murray, you see. It didn't seem possible for trust to exist on this island, for friendship to form, but we're talking without lies, we're speaking of other things other than this game we're playing. And if I have a liking and love for this one person perhaps I have the capacity to love other things. I wake with that feeling and my heart is putting it into practice and the world unfolds in front of me brand new and there is such a thing as freedom in this world and only my lack of courage will stop me from breaking out of this shit life I've made for myself here. I take these thoughts to the pool and see Murray's body drained of blood, his spirit escaped but his body slumped there and mocking any notions of a new life that I've brought here this morning! Fuck it! Fuck!

*His eyes fill with tears. He stares over at* QUINN's *body. A long pause.*

And still… I won't be beaten by what I've helped to make. (*Slight pause.*) I can't let love die. (*Pause.*) I look up from the pool at the world high above me. (*Slight pause.*) And the Earth spins around with brilliant indifference, us stuck down here, time decaying us and us staring back at fate and grimacing a little. Only love can save us. And I watch that world turning above me and I will and pray for it to happen. (*Pause.*) It rains. (*Slight pause.*) Like little lights they fall out of the grey towards the pool and maybe I'm lucky enough to catch a drop in my hand. More drops fall. (*Pause.*) And it's hope falling… and freedom… and trust… and goodness… and good dreams… and possible loves… and promise… and real care… and happiness… and sun… and affection… and friendship… and Murray… and tenderness… and love. Of course, love. The world above evaporates in its own darkness and the pool is filling with all this good rain... and it holds now all that is possible, all that will be good, Penelope. (*Slight pause*.) Your beginning... is now.

*A pause*. PENELOPE *slowly turns and looks down at* BURNS, FITZ *and* DUNNE, *as tears fill her eyes*.

Love is saved.

*Suddenly the barbecue goes up in flames. As their dream predicted, it begins from its legs and quickly spreads to the rest of the frame and the grill.*

*It is a beautiful red/orange fire and* BURNS, FITZ *and* DUNNE *stare over at it and into their death.*

*They are ready for the end.*

*The fire rages for one whole minute.* PENELOPE *turns and looks offstage and into her new future...*

*Blackout.*

*The End.*

MY FRIEND DUPLICITY

*My Friend Duplicity* was first performed as part of the 'Impossible Things Before Breakfast' staged readings at the Traverse Theatre, Edinburgh, during the Edinburgh Festival Fringe 2010. The cast was as follows:

| | |
|---|---|
| FERGAL | Niall Buggy |
| JEAN | Olga Wehrly |
| *Director* | Vicky Featherstone |

**Characters**

FERGAL, *sixty*

JEAN, *twenty-three*

FERGAL *and* JEAN *sit across from each other. A small desk sits between them. They are both seemingly at ease with each other and with themselves.*

*But unfortunately after thirty seconds –*

FERGAL. It was absolutely the most transplendent!

JEAN. What was?

FERGAL. Sorry?

JEAN. You were about to say something but I interrupted.

FERGAL. I was about to say something about what?

JEAN. I dunno.

FERGAL. You could make something up.

JEAN. Well of course I could make something up but couldn't you?

FERGAL. I prefer when you do it, Jean.

JEAN. But I was quite happy the way things were – just sitting here saying nothing.

FERGAL. Oh me too.

JEAN. But you started.

FERGAL. Maybe I wasn't happy!

JEAN. Maybe you were unhappy.

FERGAL. I might have been. Seems a bit strong, mind you. I can't really remember that strong an emotion.

JEAN. You probably felt it deep inside.

FERGAL. Yes that's very likely, Jean! You're probably right. D'you know I think I was unhappy. I'm pretty sure I was unhappy. I didn't show it on my face, did I?

JEAN. No.

FERGAL. Which is often the way I show my unhappiness. So I probably was unhappy, yeah.

JEAN. About what?

FERGAL. Oh where do I start!? My God!

JEAN. Start anywhere you want.

FERGAL. I am full of unhappiness!

JEAN. You!?

FERGAL. I must be. I said it. Or rather I didn't say it and just showed it and then I only said it after you said it. So I'm obviously desperate to share something!

JEAN. Really?

FERGAL. You picked up on it because of your womanly whatyamacallit…

JEAN. Intuition.

FERGAL. You could see inside me.

JEAN. Maybe.

FERGAL. Into my subconscious!

JEAN. Probably, yeah.

FERGAL. Beneath an exterior of…

JEAN. Passivity.

FERGAL. 'Passivity' really!!? Was that the picture on my face just then?

JEAN. What exactly are you unhappy with, Fergal?

FERGAL. Oh that's a bit forward!

JEAN. I'm just trying to move things towards…

FERGAL. I know what you're trying to do…

JEAN. So you're not going to share then?

FERGAL. Not the type of sharing that you're implying!

JEAN. The personal kind.

FERGAL. Vulgar to put a name on it, Jean!

JEAN. We can't do this for ever!

FERGAL. We could give it a bloody good go!

JEAN. It's exhausting!

FERGAL. It is exhausting but it's very important.

JEAN. And why is it important?

FERGAL. Because once we get started we're on the road to
    finishing and once we finish we're back on the road to
    starting again.

JEAN. You think we'd run out of things to talk about.

FERGAL. It's certainly feeling that way.

JEAN. How long do you think we can keep this up? This
    business of not actually talking about anything.

FERGAL. Not long, unfortunately. My energy is not what it
    was. Bloody brain!

JEAN. Are we Irish?

FERGAL. Yes of course we're Irish! In so far as I think we are,
    Jean. I mean we look Irish. It's a very personal thing but we
    are, aren't we?

JEAN. I think we are.

FERGAL. I'm certain we are.

JEAN. It would be good if we were something, I suppose.

FERGAL. What do you think would differentiate me from other
    men if I was indeed an Irish man?

JEAN. A number of things probably.

FERGAL. Like what, come on!?

JEAN. A slightly milky exterior like you've been carved from mash.

FERGAL. Check.

JEAN. An inability to swim.

FERGAL. Check.

JEAN. A masterly use of a foreign language.

FERGAL. Check-check.

JEAN. A love of the miserable.

FERGAL. For a moment I wavered there and may very well have ended up being Flemish but it's inescapable isn't it!?... In so far as you want to escape being Irish... it really is inescapable. Oh the tragedy! We're definitely Irish!

JEAN. Thank God.

FERGAL. No reason to bring God into it! We sit here and you bring God into it and suddenly...

JEAN. What?

FERGAL. Well you know suddenly it's a 'lowering'... the level of conversation has lowered and all because of God.

JEAN. Right.

FERGAL. Is that what you're trying to do, Jean?!

JEAN. Look you're the one who started talking!

FERGAL (*laughing*). I know! I know!

JEAN. Initially it was your words that broke what was previously...

FERGAL. 'Quite a nice silence.' You're right!

JEAN. We've started talking and all that can be said of any significance is that we're Irish!

FERGAL. And we can't even be certain of that!

JEAN. What were you going to see in the garden, Fergal?

FERGAL. Oh hold on a second! Come on!!

JEAN. Was it really something 'transplendent'? (*Sarcastic.*) Were you about to create something with a transplendent quality?

FERGAL. I'm not ready for that just yet, now stop it!

JEAN. This is a very small life, isn't it? Perhaps not even a life. 'Life' might be pushing it. I can't really remember how I started all this stuff but here I am and here with you and somehow we've managed to muddle through it all. But it feels 'delicate'. Don't you think what we're doing is a very delicate thing? It's not very lasting is it? We've proved that by starting over so many times. By leaving our homes and families, by travelling distances, by entering this house and climbing those stairs and finding this room and desk and just creating these moments… and how did this garden idea develop? Is there even an actual garden, Fergal?

FERGAL. Oh yes! In so far as there might be a garden but that's less important.

JEAN. How is it less important!?

FERGAL. What I'm detecting here is an anxiety, young lady!

JEAN. I am anxious… fuck…!

FERGAL. Which is normal. That's fine. We have both, in the past, now and then, felt a general lack of purpose.

JEAN. Right.

FERGAL. I remember it vividly now, way back, some time before you came even, that I too worried about my contribution to life and whether I was just adding to the general mush that life is.

JEAN. And what did you decide?

FERGAL. I think I am adding. But only as much as we all are.

JEAN. But us more than other people, surely? What practical purpose are we?

FERGAL. Entertainment!

JEAN. But are we entertaining?

FERGAL. No probably not. No one really knows and that's the beauty of what we do here, Jean. Whether we are or not is not that important to us. We are proving our existence by 'making shit up'.

JEAN. You see that's terrible!

FERGAL. Is it?

JEAN. To hear it like that. To be reminded just how…

FERGAL. Essential we are.

JEAN. I feel sick! I think I could be actually sick.

FERGAL. You've never been sick before.

JEAN. I want to die suddenly!

FERGAL. Suddenly's the best way to die. You don't want to die gradually, believe me!

JEAN (*grabbing her heart*). Oh my God this is fucking unbearable…

FERGAL. The garden was…

*A slight pause as* JEAN *waits and* FERGAL *delivers*.

Transplendent.

JEAN. Right. Okay.

FERGAL. Okay, Jean?

*A slight pause*.

JEAN (*a little sad*). Yeah. Carry on.

FERGAL. I've been walking this lawn for many years now. I have seen its natural fabric mutate into a thousand different settings around me… each garden conjuring up a different tone, a differing sense of possibility, a different and differing cast of characters that would move about me on a whim with the precision of a finely crafted automata. In short… a different garden appears to me, each day on each separate sitting at this desk right here.

JEAN (*depressed*). And to me.

FERGAL. From the puckered grass of the housing estate, to the luscious lawns of a country manor. And here I am today, Jean, dreaming up this *new* garden, defining it in a patchwork of bosquets and geometric parterres like some sculpting god presiding over all this bloody nature. I am a Baroque man in control!

JEAN. Baroque?

FERGAL. Sure is it any wonder I'm fash-uned in this eleborate flared coat with ruffled neck and sleeves, caressing my silk stockings like it were the cheek of a child.

And yet, my fellow traveller, there is a terrible consternation in my heart!

JEAN. And mine.

FERGAL (*in French*). *Un consternation terribles!* For sat here on the garden's central fountain, a fountain of such allegorical complexity that it is impossible to decipher its meaning, I am awaiting great great news!

JEAN. About what?

FERGAL. I haven't decided yet.

JEAN. About love?

FERGAL. Possibly about love.

JEAN. About death?

FERGAL. Would I be waiting for news about death while 'lounging' on a fountain in ruffled sleeves? Seems unlikely.

JEAN. Well make up something…!!

FERGAL. Great news of *love*, Jean!

JEAN. Does it involve Cynthia?

FERGAL. It does involve Cynthia!

JEAN. Then the 'great news' won't come.

FERGAL. Today it will!

JEAN. You never get that far…!

FERGAL. Today the great news will come, Jean!

JEAN. It won't, Fergal!

FERGAL. I swing my slender legs off the fountain and onto the manicured lawn, my shoulders rounding with worry. The base of my neck weighed down like an old carthorse in need of sustenance and your great news, Cynthia…!

JEAN. JUST STOP IT! ENOUGH! I can't do this any more!? Sitting here listening to your endless shit! You throw about language like it were porn. Do you have any idea how stupid all this garden business is?! To come here. To sit opposite you and talk as you do. To fart out story like some chocolatier. To fill silence with flam! I mean, Holy Christ, Fergal!

FERGAL. Now, Jean…

JEAN. I wake in the mornings with a terrible heartache. I stand in the bus the heartache compounded by people going about their lives, actually contributing to society! You know people driving other people about and driving things from here to there. Selling all manner of goods for our consumption and enjoyment. Teaching one another. Working in offices and accumulating monies for our desperate economy. And to get off the bus and to come to this house and up those stairs and into this room with your stories of Baroque fountains and ruffled sleeves, Fergal, like any of this fucking shit matters! Isn't it enough that we are!? Isn't that the most remarkable thing? Before the decoration and impossible imagination of these ridiculous things… that we get to sit at this desk and breathe and function. Isn't that amazing in itself, Fergal!?

FERGAL. No garden, then?

JEAN. We don't need the garden!

FERGAL. So what exactly are we sitting in?

JEAN. What you see!

FERGAL. And you honestly think I can just sit here in *this*?!

JEAN. Why not?

FERGAL. But talk about what, for Christ's sake?! This floor, Jean!!

JEAN. Talk about us!

FERGAL. There is no 'us'! 'Us' is imagination! 'Us' is turning this floor into grass, the lights into sky, the nothing into something. And you're wanting to give it all up and just sit here in this silence and look at the floor and marvel at the floor's construction?! Who cares about the fucking floor?! This particular floor! I don't care about the floor!

JEAN. Well perhaps I care about the floor! Every little embellishment and you're further away from truth. You start with some idea of love and you're suddenly caressing your silken tights in a Baroque garden?! WHY, FERGAL?

FERGAL. Because I am a magician! A wordsmith! What's 'truth' but some repellent-unctuous-poker-faced-twat that tiptoes into story with all the grace of a juggernaut! 'Truth!' That's your pornography, right there, young lady!

JEAN. Where do you live? When I arrive here in the mornings you're already seated and waiting for me. Do you live in this house, Fergal?

FERGAL. What's important is where I live – (*Taps his head.*) in here. You want to live in the world, Jean?! Holy Christ! Let's have a cup of tea. We haven't had our tea yet.

JEAN. I don't want tea…

FERGAL. A tea will calm you down. Help you settle into the day.

JEAN. A tea will trick me into thinking that everything is all right. When it isn't all right, Fergal. It's not even close to being right for me! Not even close! Fuck!

*JEAN breaks down and cries. A pause. FERGAL watches her.*

FERGAL. I can give you a biscuit with your tea.

*JEAN looks up at him as he places a packet of Jammy Dodgers on the desk.*

JEAN. When did we get biscuits?

*A slight pause.*

FERGAL. I picked up a packet on the way here.

*A slight pause.*

JEAN. So you do come here every morning? Just like me.

FERGAL. Yes. Of course I do.

*A slight pause.*

JEAN. Doesn't it preoccupy you… this… (*Spitting.*) *futility*?

*A long pause.* FERGAL *strains a smile.*

*Then –*

FERGAL (*Oirish accent*). Is it a cup of a tea and a biscuit
you're after then, Jeanie? (*Laughs.*) Best feeling in the world
isn't it, to wake up knowing you're Irish?! Amazing
sensation! You can throw all manner of shit at the Irish and
we'll turn it into art. The Irish are unbeatable in that respect.
We are masters of illusion, Jean. Had we the ability to truly
connect with other races you imagine the Irish could have
had a practical effect on the world. But the Irish are only
ever comfortable in their own company and the company of
oneself is a powerful thing. To retreat and live in that
isolation is to live in the community of one's imagination
and not the community of fucking people. Will you have
sugar, pet?

JEAN (*scared of him*). One sugar.

FERGAL. I'll give you two. You could do with two. If I had
two sugars I'd be spitting my molars out on this desk! Have
a bicky I bought them specially for today. Thank you, Fergal.

JEAN. Thank you, Fergal.

*A pause as* FERGAL *watches* JEAN *drink her tea.*

FERGAL. So?

*A pause.*

JEAN. What?

FERGAL. Into the garden.

JEAN (*almost breaking*). I don't want to go there...

FERGAL. Don't make me ask again. Don't you fucking dare.

*A long pause.*

JEAN *places down her tea and then* –

JEAN. And I can see you standing up from the fountain. The garden laid out in perfect symmetry between us. Nature ordered by mathematics and all beneath a canopy of blue. Your sky. Always your sky. (*Pause.*) I turn away and leave you standing there in your frock coat and ruffled sleeves and dreams of Cynthia and her 'great news'. (*Slight pause.*) I push open a wooden door and onto a busy high street. The road chocked with red buses, frustrated cars and... other people. (*Slight pause.*) I walk among them on the pavement. And I'm giddy just thinking about the amount of life and history there is in these people. The places they are going to, the conversations that have yet to happen, the expectation of an unknown day. And amazingly the whole chaos is working and I am within it and a part of the world again, Fergal. And there's no fears like before. No deep anxiety about time and place and my worth. No terrible depression asking for order. No imagination stealing me away and wrapping me up in the pretend. I'm just walking to this house on Streatley Road. To this room here. (*Slight pause.*) To you. (*Slight pause.*) And telling you that it's the morning time, Fergal. (*Slight pause.*) It's still morning and the world is open out there.

*A long pause as* FERGAL *looks at her. Then* –

FERGAL. How's the tea?

*She takes a sup.*

JEAN. Horrible.

FERGAL. You'll get used to it. Take a Jammy Dodger.

JEAN. I don't want a Jammy Dodger.

FERGAL. I bought them specially…

JEAN. I don't want to be here…

FERGAL. Take one!

JEAN. How did you buy the biscuits?

FERGAL. Entered that shop…

JEAN. Before that…

FERGAL. Why…

JEAN. How do you come here? I want to know other things! Please!!

FERGAL. I leave where I have to leave.

*A pause*. JEAN *waits*.

I've no idea what that place is any more. A room smaller than my hand and it's somewhere I close my eyes for an unknown amount of minutes. And get up then and shuffle down some stairs and push open a door clogged with post and autumn leaves and step out into London. (*Slight pause.*) My body holds the memory and I let my legs take me to the bus stop, my head bowed as always and stirring now with thoughts of this house and this room and this desk and what you and me will make today. (*Slight pause.*) I take the bus I always take, sit in the seat I always sit in and watch the bus fill with barely-there-people in their barely-there-lives. And they think I'm one of them. But inside I'm creating new ways of removing them from the world. Terrible ways. (*Slight pause.*) The bus stops and I watch you get on and stand where you always stand, Jean. And what secrets we hold from the rest. I think back to the day I brought you to this room. And we imagined things then and the things were made in front of us and we got to live and be in those worlds, didn't we? (*Slight pause.*) And day after day we come here and what colour, what unbelieveable distances we can travel to with just words, with twenty-six letters, all here at this desk. (*Slight pause.*) You step off the bus and as always I am metres behind you. You stop as you always stop. Just standing there on Kilburn High Road suspended somehow.

And I move by you unseen. And this morning I can feel the doubt coming off you... the yearning to return to a life you think 'normal' as the bus pulls past you, Jean. I can see it. (*Slight pause.*) I nip into the corner shop, buy the biscuits and quicken my stride to Streatley Road and wait as I always wait here in this room.

FERGAL *takes a Jammy Dodger out of the packet.*

We're not made for this world me and you. What does the world give us that our imaginations can't make better, Jean?

JEAN. Biscuits. (*Slight pause.*) The world makes actual things. We make the invisible... we trade in words... we make nothing you can touch.

FERGAL *places down the Jammy Dodger.*

*A long pause.*

FERGAL. And to watch Cynthia turn. And to be allowed to be in that moment. When there are billions of other moments that steal seconds from your days and give you nothing... to be given this moment with her. (*Pause.*) She turns to me and the garden, each tiny detail of the garden blossoms or breathes or colours that bit brighter maybe and certainly warms the air in the small distance between me and her. (*Slight pause.*) And it covers completely the impossible loneliness of morning time, the terrible torture of another day to be lived, the glorious shame of not having the courage to give up on it all. That turn to me lights a forgotten spark inside. It kicks my heart into life, stirs my head with the beginnings of possibility, covers the image of my abandoned hallway, my lonesome bus journeys, our pointless city. It covers everything there was and offers everything there could be. (*Closes his eyes.*) And I am with the second now. As the second is. With no past or no future but of and in the moment. And what a wonderful place to be. Without yearning, without projection... just filled with hope. (*Pause.*) Her great news may rescue me for ever... it could shape a brand-new me completely... but her walking to me is all I need. (*Slight pause.*) And I can be in the second... and I can be happy.

*Tears fall from his closed eyes as* FERGAL *remains lost in the moment and* JEAN *looks on.*

*After only ten seconds his reverie ebbs away and disappears like a drug and he is returned to the shell he is.*

JEAN. We can go, you know.

*A slight pause.*

FERGAL. We can't.

*After a long pause. The lights slowly fade out as* FERGAL *watches* JEAN *beginning to eat her biscuit.*

*The End.*

ROOM 303

*Room 303* was shown as an installation at the Galway International Arts Festival, 2014, performed by Niall Buggy.

*Room 303* was first produced as part of the Sixty-Six Books season at the Bush Theatre, London, on 13 October 2011, also performed by Niall Buggy, and directed by Madani Younis.

**Character**

MAN

*In a cheap, chaotic hotel room – a* MAN*'s voice is heard.*

On a matter of principle I would always set out to accomplish that which needs finishing. It's in my nature to finish things. I could tell you all manner of stories from my youth that would prove to you that I have that quality but you know this – of course you do – in the past I've spoken to you about this probably – it doesn't seem wildly important to go into that sort of detail just yet.

There are lots of words for what I am now – but where I am is in this room – this hotel room. At least it seems like it could be a hotel room. All indications suggest that it isn't. It's been a long time cleaned certainly. I can't see the floor. The carpet – if it is carpeted – is thick with – what exactly? I don't like looking at the floor and stay lying in the bed – or very occasionally sitting up in bed and talking as I am now – just to prove that I can sit up in a bed and talk.

I felt a twinge in my back the other day – which proves that I still have a little muscle – unfortunately. It reminds me of the years of walking – of stepping off buses – of arriving in new towns and knocking on doors and speaking then the good word to strangers – and occasionally being invited into their homes and sharing with them hot beverages and of course a saucer of biscuits. Always the confectionery! And I would leave their homes – leave them brimming with a new hope – and other men I would see leaving other houses and stepping back onto buses and travelling the country just like me with our words.

I had working muscles back then – now I'm more of a quilt in substance. Now I'm more of the bed – belong to the bed – my country is this room – my town is this mattress – my home is my head – and ordinarily I would finish a task – as you know I would – on principle I would – I would have to – but is it possible to finish this thought even – to finish this breath – this idea of me? This is the crux – as they say – of the matter.

The other day there was a fly in the room – in my country, let's keep calling it – a fat bluebottle, to give it its correct term – and he barely buzzed – so fat he was. I could see him at the far end of the country over there. He was on my papers. It was almost like he was half-reading those words – and he panted about in an asthmatic sort of way – shuffling from one line to the next – hardly looking for Enlightenment – probably looking for food matter – In here?! Anyway – he stopped his reading and seemed to be looking back at me. He then – miraculously – flew.

He was Malteser in size and an azure blue in colour and as he approached I was repulsed by this beast. How much shit had he licked in his short lifetime this fat fly? He landed where my legs are. He licked around my quilt but all the time with the intention of making his way closer to my face – which he did! And there was something in his fat swagger that suggested that he saw in me an equal. That after perusing my papers he saw in me – a beast of similar ambition to him – of similar worth – of similar purpose to him – the bastard!

*A pause.*

Surprisingly, it was never my intention to play out my last days being stared at by a fat bluebottle in a shitty hotel room. Dreams of dying were always dreams of friends or strangers I had talked to – people I had given the good word to in return for hot beverages and biscuits. I would be dying on a bed and these people would surround that bed and kind words would float down on me and ease me into my death and towards my God – my Heaven. This is the dream. This is what teases me in moments of lucidity. Ordinarily I am a man who finishes a task – I will not allow another thought to end before finding some rest!

*A slight pause.*

I will not allow that fly to wither me with his arrogance.

*A slight pause.*

Amazingly I had enough breath in me to send him toppling over this bed and into the terrible abyss of the floor. The shit! No doubt he's feeding off the remnants down there – feeding off whatever substance there is down there. But the breath does not lie! The breath tells me of my life – that I have a life still! That I must gather something from this room. That through the room's refuse I must find again what truth is! I must!

*A pause.*

What was it I stepped off those buses with? What was the thing we brought into strangers' houses? What were the good words that came from my mouth? This is the crux – as they say – of the matter. Of me.

*A pause.*

And it must be a hotel room, surely! On either side of me I can hear voices. Televisual voices with their suggestion of a world continuing – of adventure and geographies and colour. My television ceased transmission months ago. I had it running continually to drown out – difficult to put a word on it – difficult to say what exactly is emoting inside this head and needed drowning out. Anyway the fucker broke down. Some time during *Bargain Hunt* it died – gave up the ghost – kicked the televisual bucket!

And it's not a theory – I have made it a fact! It *is* a hotel room! It must be! A hotel I have often visited – we have often visited. And we would meet in the mornings at breakfast – and over our breakfasts we would again define goodness to one another – and we would write our papers and step on buses and arrive in towns and knock on doors and offer hope and drink their hot beverages. Our good words began, you see, in these hotels. In a hotel room like this one.

The theory is – the theory that must now be a fact – is that these rooms are full of us – full of men like me. It was always men like me – of my colour and type and sound. Men with my words, with my amount of words. That was the way it was – and here we are – in hotel rooms that are now our countries – in homes that are now our heads – unable to breakfast with one another and talk again of what it is we believe in any more! At least the men on either side of me have *Bargain Hunt*! At least they have the clatter of daytime television to stave off what I must now face here alone in the silence, in the darkness with a fat bluebottle for company! My God!

*A long pause and only his breath.*

And it's something I don't like to do – have not done for some time now – but must.

*A slight pause.*

Do it!

*A pause.*

I look down from the bed. Down at what was the floor…

…and pictures there – of a house I was taken home to and sisters and brothers in their best clothes and a dog who once shared this house and a garden crisp in black and white but a yellow car – and my father with sleeves and trousers rolled up, a cigarette in his mouth not yet lit and me in his arms.

And scenes in a new house with another garden and the gate that led to the open road and the feeling still of the freshly cut grass tickling the backs of my legs as I'm sat under an inflatable paddling pool with Sinead such-and-such kissing me or rather plunging her tongue into my mouth and telling me it was called 'kissing'.

And faster the images come and fill the floor with smells of youth and half-dreamt stories of Dollymount Strand and the sea in front and breaking hearts and pulverising livers and the smell of sex in every breath and an idea of the world and my involvement in that world and burning friendships and terrible indifference and insatiable lusts and sweet vodka and every day boredom.

And amongst the remnants a clearer more isolated me – a broken self-hating me – an insignificant vocally retarded young man who continues to show half-notions of himself and proclaims half-truths of himself and sells them as gospel to strangers who cram together and nod barely.

And through the clatter of my younger years and falling deeper now into the floor and into the quick burn of happiness of my later years – deluded in its ridiculous importance but briefly it seems rescued – rescued by His words.

And joined to others and breakfasts and bus journeys and spreading those words like new air until all there is is God's truth and my body ageing.

*A pause.*

That truth now forgotten. Gone. Completely.

*A pause.*

And the remnants clear a little further – fall away – evaporate around one another – the carpet disintegrating with nothing to hold it now – memories disappearing as a larger breath takes them.

*A pause.*

I look down from this bed into the big space beneath me…

…and there…

…I can see a man lying in his bed… lying beneath his quilt… And he's staring back up at me.

And he too is talking with frightened eyes. Holding on for a few seconds more of life – like I too hold on for life. And his words I can't hear.

*A slight pause.*

I don't know what it is he's saying. No one knows.

*A slight pause.*

Not even he.

*The End.*

# BALLYTURK

*Ballyturk* was first performed at the Black Box Theatre, Galway, as part of the Galway International Arts Festival on 14 July 2014 in a production by Landmark Productions and Galway International Arts Festival, with the following cast:

| | |
|---|---|
| 1 | Cillian Murphy |
| 2 | Mikel Murfi |
| 3 | Stephen Rea |
| VOICES | Eanna Breathnach, Niall Buggy, |
| | Denise Gough, Pauline McLynn |
| GIRL | Orla Ní Ghríofa, Aisling Walsh |

| | |
|---|---|
| *Director* | Enda Walsh |
| *Designer* | Jamie Vartan |
| *Lighting Designer* | Adam Silverman |
| *Sound Designer* | Helen Atkinson |
| *Composer* | Teho Teardo |

The production subsequently toured to the Olympia Theatre, Dublin, Cork Opera House, and the National Theatre, London.

## Characters

1

2

3

*A seven-year-old* GIRL

*A very large room – too large.*

*Essentially it appears to be a one-roomed dwelling. There's a sleeping area, a toilet and shower area, there are old wardrobes, battered wall units and what looks like a single pull-down bed. The oddest thing is that all this furniture has been pushed against the two side walls making a large area in the middle where there is nothing but a tiny camping table (with a tablecloth) and two kitchen chairs (cushioned).*

*The back wall looks vast – its painted surface white and powdery to the touch. On this wall a large mustard curtain is drawn – where possibly a window is.*

*The two side walls are of similar colour and texture but these walls are covered with stacked furniture and drawings. From where we sit it looks like a child's drawings of people's faces and animals and buildings and maps and countryside…*

*There is something unquestionably rural about this dwelling. It is both comfortable and austere – clean and shambolic. Though it isn't pushed on first viewing – tonally everything is dark and pale.*

*But firstly – we're in darkness.*

*Music plays for some moments.*

*A light very slowly fades up on the face of a man in his mid-thirties wearing a 1970s red hurling helmet.*

*We'll call him* 1.

*Out of breath, aglow in sweat and* 1 *is desperately finishing something epic –*

1. …and dawn shining now. (*Slight pause.*) It warms the air around him and pushes back all that was yesterday. (*Pause.*) And in his mouth he tastes the drink from last night, beneath his nails the dirt from Marnie's garden, in his jacket the

smells of her new perfume, the dust of glass from her window. His eyes close and the noises he carries are churned into one another and pounding out now into the dawn. They crash over their hills and through the woods and down into the stream that runs through Ballyturk.

*A breath in the darkness – 1 barely flinches.*

Marnie Reynolds would be waking up to her burnt kitchen – she'd smell the smoke from beneath her new perfume and hear the embers and she'd know that it was him. In the dawn he is barely the man he was yesterday. Poisonous his envy. Inescapable his crime. And the air is whispering still – (*Slight pause.*) 'Larry Aspen has a knife. He will never see the full morning.'

*A pause and silence now.*

 *It's over.*

*1 looks upwards.*

Nothing.

*The sound of crisps being eaten. He then turns to his left –*

*– the lights go up on the whole space.*

*Standing very close to 1 is a man in his mid-forties dressed only in his underpants and socks – covered head to toe in talcum powder. He is sporting a fantastic ginger mullet – the talcum powder accentuating its redness.*

*This is 2.*

*He stops eating his crisps, saves a few and carefully folds them up into a tiny square. He unzips a small pocket in the inside of his underpants and places the crisps inside.*

*He looks back up at 1.*

2. I probably should have dressed.

1 (*cold*). I don't think that would have helped.

2. It caught me off-guard.

1. It happens sometimes.

1 *looks down at the knife he's holding.*

*With a Dustbuster,* 2 *sucks up the embers around* 1*'s feet. When he's finished, he stands up.*

2. Have we eaten properly?

1. We should.

1 *turns away and walks over to the stage-right wall with the knife. He stands by a chest of drawers. Inexplicably he hops twice like a bunny rabbit and mimes stabbing someone. Frightening himself, he quickly opens up the top drawer and throws the knife inside.*

*He takes the hurling helmet off – gives it a withering look – and places it on the chest of drawers.*

2 *sees this.*

*From a shelf,* 1 *takes down a clock. He begins to wind it slowly and the action of this visibly calms him.*

2 *meanwhile has picked up a red balloon (there are three other red balloons in the space). Over on stage left he's slowly flicking through a box of records (45s) in their white sleeves but without their covers. He does this with great concentration.*

1*'s meditative clock-winding has been interrupted as suddenly he's seen something.*

*It is something invisible to us – something hovering in the air in front of him.*

*He holds his breath so as not to scare it. Without looking at the shelf – he slowly places back the clock.*

*BANG!*

2 *has burst the balloon he was holding. He continues to flick through the records.*

*His breath still held and* 1 *really needs to breathe now – his body's contracting a little – his face is straining. There's nothing for it – he takes a sharp intake of breath a little too loud.*

*2's found the record he's been looking for.*

*1 concentrates on that something in front of him. His hand is primed, he widens his eyes – and reaches out in a flash and grabs a fly.*

*2 carefully checks the record for scratches.*

*1, keeping the fly secret from 2, feels the sensation of the fly in his hand. It is a huge momentous find – his brain and heart may explode. Slowly he raises his hand to his ear.*

*2 does not hear – but we hear what 1 hears – the buzzing of the fly – extremely loud.*

*1 lowers his hand quickly and the sound cuts.*

*2 ceremoniously places the single on the record player.*

*1 is unsure of what to do with the fly – he's excited/panicked. He goes to show it to 2 but instinctively decides against it. Maybe he should hold it in his mouth or his pocket – suddenly he has a better idea.*

*He walks quickly to a small cuckoo clock on the stage-right wall – opens it – and places the fly inside and shuts the little door.*

*The record blasts out ABC's 'The Look Of Love'.*

*1 stares at the cuckoo clock and backs away from it.*

*2 opens a wardrobe door.*

*Fourteen seconds into the song and suddenly 1 turns and rushes over and takes out a pair of trousers from that wardrobe – 2 steps into the trousers while taking a shirt out of the wardrobe. In one movement 2 is in the shirt – both of them buttoning the shirt's buttons.*

*1 races across the space as 2 opens a drawer in a chest of drawers.*

*1 flings open another wardrobe and dozens of shoes topple out. He drops to his knees and tries to find a matching pair.*

*2 is trying on a succession of jumpers and cardigans very fast. 1 returns with a pair of runners. 2 steps into them and opts for a bright-yellow golfing jumper. Brand new he removes it from its cellophane wrapper and flings it over his shoulders.*

*At 1:04 in the song, he's dressed. Good.*

*1 races to the fridge as 2 races to a cabinet in the kitchen area. 1 returns with milk and two bowls – while 2 returns with two boxes from the Kellogg's Variety Pack and two spoons.*

*They sit – open their cereals – pour the milk and eat – sharing each other's cereal every other mouthful.*

*They finish and tidy away the breakfast things back in the kitchen.*

*As they do this – 2 is undressing 1. When he is down to his underpants he is ready to step into the shower – which he does. There's a half-door where he drapes his underpants over.*

*1 showers in a woefully weak shower.*

*2 does some stretches and golf swings (from somewhere he's picked up a golf club – a titanium-made 3 wood).*

*At 2:40 in the song – the shower is over and 1 steps out of the shower in an elasticated* Star Wars *beach towel that hangs over his shoulders. He dries himself, puts on his underpants and drops the towel.*

*2 covers him in talcum powder – firing it at him from washing-up bottles.*

*They both run over to the dressing area. 2 flings open the wardrobe and puts trousers on 1 as 1 opens the chest of drawers and takes out a red T-shirt.*

*2 has put socks on 1 somehow and now runs over to the shoe wardrobe.*

*He throws open the door and tons of yellow ladies' shoes topple out. He tries to find a matching pair.*

*1 has a little rest.*

*2 runs back with a pair of ladies' shoes. 1 steps into them, walks around, hates them and kicks them off.*

*He goes to the freezer and takes out a pair of runners and places them on. Perfect.*

*The song ends as the alarm clock goes off.*

*2 saunters over to the alarm clock like a tiger (it was the one that 1 was winding) and switches it off – winds it for three seconds and puts it back on the shelf – when 1 is upon him fast and a little anxious –*

1. So to finish what I started earlier –

2. Right.

1. – there was a terrible – whatyacallit – a terrible?

2. Wind?

1. No a terrible – it's a feeling – a sensation –

2. A draft?

1. It's like a draft but more overriding.

2. A breeze?

1. Less of a breeze and even more invisible.

2. A waft?

1. Tell me something of no importance and the word will come to me guaranteed.

2. Francie Lyon's head was twenty inches wider than his neck – from a distance he looked like a wandering yield sign.

1. Forebodance!

2. Foreboding.

1. Foreboding?

2. Foreboding.

1. A terrible foreboding!

2. Right.

2 *picks up another balloon*.

1. And it was everywhere this feeling – not unlike the wind – but more surreptitious than the wind.

2. Like a draft?

1. It was exactly like a draft! And it came to me as I slept just then.

2. And it affected you?

1. It darkened me, yeah. You see I was having a dream about a small animal – the thing that we call a bunny rabbit.

2. A cuddly one?

1. He was lovely yeah.

2. Was he coloured cream?

1. No he was creamy white actually.

2. Awwwww.

1. So he was out shopping in the shops for groceries –

2. As rabbits do.

1. – and he had just taken a shopping bag out of his car when he heard a voice from across the street calling him – it was his brother.

2. Another bunny?

1. He came from a long line of bunnies.

2. Okay.

1. Our bunny – the creamy-white one – hopped across the road – the busy road –

2. Already foreboding.

1. I know, right!

2. Was he struck by a car!?

1. He wasn't no.

2. Was it a truck?

1. No.

2. Was he very nearly struck by a vehicle?

1. No he wasn't at all. He made it unharmed to the other side of the road – whereupon his brother pulled a knife on him and pushed it into his head. Out of nowhere, no reasoning at all, no history.

2. Well that's family for ya.

1. No sense to it but it seemed, you know –

2. Inevitable.

1. Exactly.

    *BANG!*

    *2 explodes the balloon.*

    We've probably talked about this but it's worth having the conversation again. Is it at all possible – let's use the example of a bunny rabbit seeing as we're here already – though I could be talking about me or you…

2. Let's not talk about us.

1. Bunnies are a little more arbitrary.

2. They are.

1. Do bunnies definitely have legs by the way?

2. We decided on five.

1. Five?!

2. Yeah I know.

1. Is five enough?

2. I think so.

1. Anyway! Is it at all possible for a bunny to carry with them the full spectrum of characteristics at all times during the day as they hop about their business?

2. Absolutely it is!

1. Seriously?!

2. Oh definitely!

1. The thought of a bunny being innocent-kind-affectionate-generous-welcoming-shy-reserved-cold-calculating-devious-cruel-malevolent-murderous and savage all at the same time – it's a terrifying thought, isn't it?!

2. A malevolent bunny is terrifying, yeah.

1. I mean, how would you know?

2. How would you know what you were dealing with.

1. I don't think bunnies should be given that complexity.

2. No.

1. It feels like it might be stifling for something so fluffy.

2. You're right yeah.

1. Grand for us human beings but a little too tangled for an animal.

2. Human beings can cope with a little more complexity, all right.

1 (*like it's hilarious*). It is tiring, mind you!

2. Yeah it's exhausting – but to think if you were born a chair! And just how restricted and dull the life of a chair must be!

1. Right.

*1 slowly walks over to the cuckoo clock and the hidden fly.*

2.  So really the luck to have been born a human being – to see what we say and to experience people and places and very occasionally moments of miracle…

*1 adopts a ridiculous pose where he has casually placed his ear against the clock.*

*As he does this we hear the very loud buzzing of an angry fly as 2 yabbers on about stuff we thankfully can't hear.*

*1 removes his ear from the clock, the fly noise is cut and –*

…I mean it crushes me when I think what a wall must live through!

1  (*distant*). Right.

2. Just standing there! And yeah it serves a purpose and it has a stoic quality but nothing ever changes for a wall! Smaller things can get away with reserve but a wall looks terribly awkward in its silence!

*Suddenly a loud muffled noise is heard behind the stage-right wall.*

1. Sshhhh!

*They freeze and stare at the wall – and as they do we hear clearly two voices on the other side.*

VOICE 1 (*an old man*). And you saw Jimsy, you said?

VOICE 2 (*a young woman*). Oh I did ya?

*2 has grabbed the red hurling helmet.*

VOICE 1. And how did he look?

VOICE 2. He looked fuckin' terrible.

VOICE 1. 'Fuckin' terrible'? – Jaynee!

VOICE 2. Just like you imagine an old man would look riddled with cancer.

*2 places the helmet back on 1's head.*

VOICE 1. Ohh is he riddled?

VOICE 2. From head to toe he is.

VOICE 1. I thought it was only the left side of his brain.

1. Hello in there!

VOICE 2. Well it got in through his left ear –

VOICE 1. Right.

VOICE 2. – but then journeyed west –

VOICE 1. Okay.

VOICE 2. – only to travel south.

VOICE 1. My God.

VOICE 2. Whereupon it riddled him.

VOICE 1. He should have worn a hat.

1. That's what I was going to say!

VOICE 2. Did you eat that egg I gave ya, by the way?

VOICE 1. Oh I did yeah! Jesus it was divine! A magnificent
    yoke!

VOICE 2. You love eggs.

1. I love eggs!

VOICE 1. Oh I worship an egg. I do often daydream of
    changing shape like that of the Greek Minotaur but in
    chicken-form.

VOICE 2. Okay.

VOICE 1. Happily I would sit around laying eggs into my hand
    and eating them religiously. And although devouring one's
    unfertilised young may seem completely disgusting to some
    people, my conscience would be forever beaten by the
    promise of an eggy stomach!

VOICE 2. I'll bring you an egg from Drench's tomorrow so.

VOICE 1. Oh good girly!

> 1 *hammers the wall.*

1   (*calls*). Hello in there! Hello…!

> *There's no response.*

> *2 is now holding the last two balloons pretending they're
> weights. 2 watches* 1 *– something's going to happen –*

Is that a new jumper?

2. 'Tis-new-yeah.

1. Are you going to wear it like that?

2. Like what?

1. Like – over the shoulders.

2. I might do – I haven't decided.

1. It's good with your hair.

2. Thanks very much.

1. I wish I had better hair.

2. Hair's a great companion and level-headed too – to think what it has to put up with.

1. What's that?

2. Pushed from the inside so that what it shows on the outside is already dead.

1. Seriously?

2. Absolutely.

1. Imagine the will that takes. To continue growing all that time knowing that your dead bits are being manipulated into new life. I couldn't do it.

2. Me neither.

1. If the conditions were right, I might be able to do it.

2. Yeah if the conditioning was right, you might.

1. I might draw a picture of that image later...

2. That'd be lovely...

*2 quickly gets to the back of* 1 *and holds him – as* 1 *collapses.*

1 *convulses violently/quietly.*

*The seizure stops after ten seconds.*

*His body now still – and* 2 *holds* 1 *for a few more seconds before letting him go.*

1 *looks at him. He takes off his helmet and hands it to* 2.

1. Thanks.

2. Okay.

1. Isn't it time yet?

2. Lemme check…

1. No no no let me…!

*2's walking to the cuckoo clock –*

2. Don't be silly!

*2 goes to open the little door but 1 slaps his hand away.*

1. Let me, I said!!

*2 looks at 1 and whacks him hard on the forehead with his knuckles.*

*It hurts – both of them.*

2. Sorry!

1. Sure.

2. A little too –

1. – zealous.

2. Right – sorry!

*1 and 2 walk away from the clock but 2 quickly doubles back and opens the little door.*

*The fly flies out and 2 swipes at it with the golf club a few times.*

*He throws the club to the side, claps his hands and crushes it.*

*A pause as they both feel the moment.*

*1 and 2 look down at the dying fly on the floor – 2 quickly stands on it.*

*Then –*

1. What was that?

2. Dust.

1. I didn't know that dust buzzed.

2. It can do yeah.

*A slight pause.*

1. I didn't know it could grow wings.

*The cuckoo shoots out of the clock and calls loudly three times.*

*On the third time, 1 goes to the curtain on the back wall and holds the rope to pull it open.*

*2 picks up three darts and faces the curtain two metres from it.*

*1 opens the curtain with a –*

Whoosh!

*Written in red-neon Celtic calligraphy, the word 'BALLYTURK' noisily flickers on. Underneath it are dozens of small drawn faces.*

*2 closes his eyes and fires a dart into the wall. 1 checks where it stuck.*

(*Through a microphone.*) Larry Aspen.

*2 fires another dart at the faces.*

Joyce Drench.

*2 whispers 'Cody Cody' over and over and fires his last dart.*

Cody Finnington.

2. YES!

*1 closes the curtains.*

*2 turns towards us, puts on the yellow jumper (it's tight) and composes himself.*

*He slowly raises his hand upwards. He's holding a comb.*

*1 cranks a large lever and the stage is plunged into darkness but for a small light on 2's face.*

*As 2 slowly combs his hair –*

He stands on Moyne Street his heart paused, all his small
yesterdays huddled around each other – for soon they would
mean nothing – soon all his days would be scratched out –
'cause today would be the first day of his last days. Today
the people of Ballyturk would make it so.

*The world of Ballyturk is told almost like film noir – lights
cut through the darkness and catch detailed glimpses of what
1 and 2 are creating in the moment.*

*1 is seen in the shadows.*

1. Somethin' about that jumper and how he stands there
   expecting people to orbit his greatness has Larry Aspen
   itchin' to take his piece of him. Cody restin' a fag in his lips
   like he's suckin' the feckin' thing –

2. Larry.

1. Shockin' day, isn't it?

2. It is yeah…

1. Just when you tink it might –

2. – it doesn't yeah.

1. It's like it can't decide itself.

2. I know Larry, yeah.

1. Off to deliver a little present to Marnie Reynolds, Cody.

2. Ah that's nice.

1. I can't say I ever saw a yella jumper.

2. Haven't ya ever?

1. Never no.

2. Oh right.

1. Browns and blacks are more of what you expect round here.

2 (*narrates*). His grubby fingers twitchin' about Marnie's
   present.

1. Sorta-pops-outaya-that-jumper.

2. His polished shoes doin' a two-step on the kerb.

1. It's-sorta-you-not-you.

2. That smirk crackin' into a gape.

1. What the feck are ya wearin' yella for?!

2. Walk away.

1 (*calling after him*). I HATE FECKIN' YELLA!

2. Walk away from Larry with the jumper tighter around my body – the coins in my hand remindin' me of Joyce Drench's Emporium of Groceries.

1. Cody!

2. Walk through Ballyturk and the birds are flyin' from the woods.

1 *opens a wardrobe and a corridor of light in which birds noisily fly* –

They take to the rooftops and caw all manner of nonsense downwards. Can see them ahead outside Deasy's and they're feedin' on last night's chips. Nearin' them now and they scatter 'cept one. A fat bird jabs at a burger – his hate for me and my jumper taken out on that skinny slab of meat.

1. Feckin' yella!

2. They gather on the wires and look down as I walk onwards and into Joyce's with thoughts of a glass of milk back home and maybe a lovely Hobnob.

*Sound of a door 'dinging' open.*

*A light slowly comes up on 1 standing high – he's slowly putting tins of peas onto a high narrow shelf full of tins of peas.*

1. Her tiny feet on the ladder-steps and Joyce Drench is packin' away tins of peas. Her head full of last night's bingo, her agonising defeat to Marnie Reynolds and her own reliance on lime in lager. She hears him enter – the smoke on his breath visible before he is.

2. Mornin' Joyce.

1. Mornin' Cody.

2. The fridge in the back of her shop groaning and callin' me downwards. I stand tinkin' about my mottled life and lookin' at her yogurts.

1. And she starin' at his jumper like he's King F-in' Midas.

2. Any semi-skimmed milk?

1. Somethin' about those words, about that jumper – somethin' in how he stands there, in how he talks, narrows her little shop, cheapens it and marks her down as less than him. (*Slight pause*.) Behind the eggs!

2. Walk back with the milk and she's stood there in her pink slippers with scorn cut into her craggy face.

1. I never seen a yella jumper before – not somethin' you'd ever see – not common.

2. No not common.

1. Not normal in any sense.

2. Maybe-not-no.

1. What is it you have against brown, Cody?

2. I've nothin' against brown actually.

1. Brown's a perfectly good colour.

2. I know it is yeah.

1. It hasn't got the show of a yella but brown's a great base for a man –

2. Okay.

1. – as is whole milk. Sure what's semi-skimmed but the anaemic cousin to the full-fat…

2. Right well thanks Joyce!

1. From where I'm standin' I'm not hearin' thanks at all!

2. I walk away.

1 (*barks*). Not even close, Cody!!

*Sound of a door 'dinging' closed.*

2. Walk on –

1. Not close!

2.  – and back out to Moyne Street with the semi-skimmed as a silent companion. The birds have brought the cats and the streets start packin' with the smell of kitty-cat and their endless keening. Walk over the cats with the birds divin' from the wires and snappin' at my new jumper! All is birds and cats and feathers and fur and what a curse to step out into this town…!

*A cacophony of horrible sounds as 2 walks over the cats – and the birds peck holes in his unfortunate jumper.*

And now from behind their windows I can hear them start over again. And they're spinnin' tales about me and the yellow jumper. Sniggerin' into cups of tea and draggin' up other half-truths that I never stood up to before! If I could find that voice and see those words and tell them how it was, how it always is for Cody…!

1. Oh mother of shite!!

2. And Larry Aspen's stood bangin' on Marnie's door, clutchin' that little gift –

1. Whatcha wearin' yella for?!

2. Walk past and fast now!

1 (*hammering*). Come out and take a-look at dis Marnie-love!

2. I forget all thoughts of milk and biscuits –

1. A pressie, Marnie!

2.  – and march with the town shovin' me t'wards the woods. To the woods – to the woods – to the woods!

*A moment of rest and through the music – the sound of a breeze through the trees can be heard.*

And hidden and safe now. Let that quiet sound take me there. (*Slight pause.*) My shoes in the soft floor and for a heartbeat it feels like I'm the only man alive.

*He takes out the ends of his crisps and eats them.*

*But then –*

And that's when it starts. The jumper moves in on me. It squeezes around my skin and harder it pushes – and in doing so it begins to push up all this hate I have for the town of Ballyturk. It forms inside streams of sharp thoughts – till I'm shoutin' into the trees these years of trapped and swallowed gutless words! But trapped no more! For an hour I shout myself hoarse – and with each moment a better me – a stronger me!

1. All that hate for Ballyturk it rises from his throat and into the branches to somewhere safe it goes. But the birds are up there waitin' and listenin' and the birds will have their say…

2. And walk back through the woods with all my spite spat out – my body lighter for all of that. And soon to be back home with the biscuits and the not-too-full-fat-milk, Cody! Soon to be safe and plugged into ease…

1. But then.

2. And feck it then.

1. A black cloud sits down on Ballyturk.

*The sound of noisy birds gathering overhead –*

2. The people are fallin' out of houses, their heads bent upwards –

1. – the birds are pickin' their time till he walks into town – and they speak those birds! They speak!

2. From the sky they speak all my hate.

*1 has grabbed the microphone and mixed to make him sound half-bird –*

1. 'And what are those people but less than spit! Less than scum! And hardly born but cut from animals and reared as pigs! And ignorant fucking bits of muck – and uglier than sin the people of Ballyturk – and faces pulled from mash potato and bodies carved from gelatinous buckets of phlegm…!'

2. And the bad people of Ballyturk their heads bent me-wards –

1. CODY!

2. – they walk. They walk fast!

1. CODY!

2. The yellow jumper pins me down and unable to run they are on me now! And there is fists and boots and knives and teeth and tearin' of skin and pulling of innards and stamping and no no no no no NO NO NO NO…

*Music and sounds swell to noise. The space seems to shake until –*

*Everything suddenly stops and a single light snaps down on 2 as he looks upwards.*

*A sudden blast of air almost sucks him off his feet and for a brief three seconds it is the most glorious release.*

*We crash back into the room's normal state – and how harsh and bare everything looks now.*

*Then –*

1. Nice.

2. Thanks.

*Blackout – for four seconds –*

*Lights up with the alarm and 1 and 2 hop out of the pull-down bed.*

*2 walks over to the records.*

*1 is walking over to the alarm clock when he stops dead.*

*There's a small flower (a marigold) in a flowerpot on the shelf in front of the clock.*

*He slowly approaches it like it was a bomb.*

*2 has found the record he wants. He turns and sees 1 – he sees the flower.*

*1 takes the helmet off the chest of drawers and places it on.*

1 *must reach around the flower to turn off the clock. He does this.*

*The two men stand looking at the flower. How did it get there?*

2 *turns away and puts on the record as* 1 *backs away from the marigold.*

*Suddenly Blancmange's 'Living On the Ceiling' is heard.*

*Thirteen seconds into the song and the two men turn in to one another and begin to dance a country-western two-step.*

*They're good.*

*As it progresses, the formalities of the dance give over to new steps and improvisation.*

*At around 1:30,* 1 *convulses and the song suddenly stops.*

*Suddenly another very loud muffled noise is heard. They both look to the stage-left wall.*

1. Sshhhh!

*They freeze and stare at the wall – and as they do we hear clearly another two voices behind the wall.*

VOICE 3 (*woman*). But ya look great – ya look absolutely wonderful!

VOICE 4 (*a young effeminate man*). Oh I feel wonderful. I feel invigorated actually!

1. Hello in there!

VOICE 3. It's like there's somethin' in ya – like a soul or somethin' coming out of your body.

VOICE 4. You know I think that's what was unlocked! Not that I didn't have a soul before the massage but the penetration was second to none.

VOICE 3. And from a woman – Jesus Christ?!

VOICE 4. I know, right! She wasn't a petite woman now.

VOICE 3. Was it Wags Mickles?

VOICE 4. In a certain light she was rather mannish looking and her hands were the hands of a strangler –

VOICE 3. But she realigned ya, nonetheless?!

VOICE 4. Oh she did yeah yeah yeah! Sure the health centre's a godsend!

1. There's a health centre!

VOICE 3. Well it's the only wheelchair ramp in town.

VOICE 4. Is it?

VOICE 3. The church's wheelchair ramp was torn up back in the winter.

VOICE 4. Jesus I never knew that.

VOICE 3. There was a terrible ground frost the morning of Collette Chinigan's funeral.

VOICE 4. Yeah right.

*1 looks at the flower, 2 looks at the bed.*

VOICE 3. Her three sons are ferocious alcoholics as you well know and apparently they were green on their feet as they carried their mother's remains out on their narrow shoulders. Sure poor Dinty Chinigan slipped on the icy wheelchair ramp – Collette came down on him hard – the casket's brass handles opening his head – like a fork being pushed into a boiled potato. To save on the cost of another casket they just lay Dinty's body on top of his mother's. Buried them both – like a Twix bar.

1 *(calls)*. Hello! Can you hear us?!

*Silence.*

It really does sound like there's someone there!

*2 faces the microwave whose light is on – it pings loudly. He opens it and takes out two miniature steaming hot dogs.*

2. So I don't want to build this up.

1. Build what?

2.  What I'm about to say? I'm a little torn as to how I should start talkin' about it.

1.  Why's that?

2.  Because it may or may not be important.

1.  Why does that matter?

2.  You're right, it doesn't matter.

    *2 quickly measures the hot dogs and hands one to 1.*

    *1 eats it in a second.*

    I had a dream about your bunny rabbit just then.

1.  Seriously?

2.  Deadly serious.

1.  The five-legged one?

2.  All bunnies have five legs.

1.  So what happened?

2.  Well it was before he went shopping for groceries, before his stabbing at the paws of his own brother – it was the morning of that same day.

1.  How did you know it was that day?

2.  It had that foreboding you talked about.

1.  Forebodance.

2.  Foreboding.

1.  Foreboding?

2.  Foreboding. It had that forebodance.

1.  Foreboding.

2.  Right.

1.  So what was he doing?

2.  He was at home brushing his teeth in his bathroom. His wife was sitting on the toilet and telling him all the things he needed to buy from Drench's.

*Unconsciously* 1 *has taken off the helmet and handed it to* 2.

1. Was she a rabbit?

2. No she was a woman.

1. Right.

2. You could tell they had a wonderful marriage just by how she was listing all the food they needed.

1. A lot of carrots?

2. Masses of carrots. And although it was a perfectly normal scene of a woman sitting on a toilet talking to her rabbit husband about vegetables – it already had a gathering darkness about it.

1. Bigger than what happened to him later? (*Makes the stabbing motion.*)

2. It was something to do with me and you, I think.

*A pause.*

1. Feck it, I don't feel well...

2. How'd ya mean?

1. I feel funny.

2 *quickly places the helmet back on* 1.

2. Well sit down!

1. I don't want to sit!

2. Stand then.

1. Standing's not helping!

2. You could crouch.

1. Am I breathing any differently?

2. You're using your nose and mouth.

1. Right...

2. At the same time.

1. Okay…

2. Excessively. It's doing odd things to your face.

    1 *retches*.

1. My hand's shaking!

2. You're making it shake!

1. I'm making this one shake but this is being shook by something else.

2. By what?!

1. By fear! What d'you tell me that dream for?!

2. I didn't know you were scared of bunnies!

1. It isn't the bunnies!! If even in sleep we're talkin' the same thing – where's the space?

2. What ya mean?!

1. Sleep is freedom!

2. Freedom from what!? Why would you use that word…!?

    2 *slaps* 1 *in the face, hard*.

    1 *immediately calms. He looks at his hand*.

1. It's stopped.

2. It's normal to feel nervous when you've lost yourself, it can happen but it passes.

1. Right. Thank you.

2. Sure.

    1 *takes off his helmet*.

    *Then –*

1. How many other things have wings that I didn't know had wings?

    2 *doesn't answer*.

I thought we knew everything there was to know. (*Slight pause*.) There was that story you told me once about that boy who'd seen a small cloud out on a lake – and it was in the shape of his sister – and he rowed out there towards her. He rowed with their past falling away behind him. (*Slight pause*.) He's sitting in a bath and his hands are holding the soap – and she's across from him singing something – and much later and through leaves and their hands are moving towards berries – and sitting then and eating those berries. And the two of them playing – and falling asleep then in a car – and asleep still and lifted and laid down together in the same bed – and just barely awake and already talking fully to one another. (*Slight pause*.) He rowed that boat towards that image of her standing there – and closer – and of course not her – and her image not made up of cloud but something else, you said – and you said how that something else 'buzzed' – how its 'wings' moved it over the water towards him and the boat – and when that boy stood up and went to hold her – it was 'flies' was the word. (*Slight pause*.) Don't you remember saying all that? Saying that word. (*Slight pause*.) So that's what it was.

2. What?

1. 'It' – earlier.

2. It was dust.

   *A pause*.

1. It feels like we may be less of what we were in a place we don't know wholly now. (*Slight pause*.) Do you feel that way?

   *A slight pause*.

2. Barely.

1. 'Barely' is enough.

   *A pause*.

2. So ya ready?

1. Okay.

2. Go.

1 *starts listing Ballyturk people as 2 takes on their image.*

1. Larry Aspen. Jimsy Behan.

*Music.*

Suzy Clutch. Nags Mickles. Boxer Brady. Phyliss Brady. Tina and Tony Brady. Father Garrington. Dinty Chinigan. Barbara Muffing-Field. Lexy Stafford. Honey Chasty. Clifford Cleary. Marnie Reynolds. Big-Mick Langley. Smidgee Coates. Nana Coates. Cody Finnington. Ferdy Oppington....

1 *continues to call out names we don't hear as 2 continues to pose as these people.*

*It is endless.*

*Sad.*

*After thirty seconds of this, the cuckoo clock sounds.*

1 *and 2 go to the clock and look at it. On the third call, 2 turns and goes to the curtain and opens it.*

*The music continues as 1 throws the three darts into the faces and 2 calls their names through the microphone (we don't hear him).*

1 *turns to us as 2 closes the curtain and pulls the lever – a single light coming down on 1.*

1 *shoots up his hand. He's holding a large pair of women's spectacles. He looks up at his hand and it's starting to shake again.*

She stands on Moyne Street... (*Stops.*) I can't.

2 *holds and calms 1.*

*Sound of a door 'dinging' open.*

*A light comes up on 1 standing high – he's slowly putting tins of peas onto a high narrow shelf full of tins of peas. He's taken on Joyce Drench.*

Her tiny feet on the ladder-steps and Joyce Drench is packin' away tins of peas. Her head full of last night's bingo, her agonising defeat to Marnie Reynolds and her own reliance on lime in lager. She hears her enter – the scent in the air visible before she is.

2. Mornin' Joyce.

1. Mornin' Marnie.

2. Some bingo last-night-all-together-wasn't-it?

1. 'Twas, yeah.

2. I was only saying that to Larry when he popped inta me this mornin' to make plans for our special-evenin'-dis-evenin'. You might be able to detect the new perfume that Larry purchased as a little present for me.

1. Perfume right.

2. It's called, 'Just Maybe' – and I tink that's a very appropriate name for what me and Larry might accomplish tonight. I'm talkin' about a delicious dinner in The Rusty Anchor in celebration of Cody's mauling – followed by a midnight stroll by the stream – and who knows – maybe an ol'-fumble-in-da-woods!

1. What is it you need, Marnie?

2. When your perfume wafts in front of you a course that could navigate the most miserable of towns – the only thing in need of benefaction is the interior.

1. And what's that then?

2. A packet of Polos. Thanks Joyce!

1. From where I'm standin' I'm not hearin' thanks at all!

2. I walk away.

1 (*barks*). Not even close, Marnie!!

*Sound of a door 'dinging' closed.*

2. Walk on –

1. Not close!

2. – and back out to Moyne Street with the Polo mints as a silent companion. Ballyturk lurches in silence – the buildings slumped against one another like five-day-old drunks – they turn me in on myself and have me recallin' those romantic words shared between me and Larry that very mornin' –

1. People have said that your scent could rejuvenate the most fetid of toilets – like your floral fragrance was regurgitated from the mouths of flowers and spat onto your delicate neck.

2. Thank you, Larry.

1. But travelling on my travels – I happened upon a lady shop and purchased that bottle of perfume – on the off-chance that if I gave it to you outta respect and love – that after a meat supper in The Rusty Anchor – we could stroll hand in hand through the woods over the hills and allow our passion to create new languages for themselves – if you get my meanin', pet.

2. I walk through Ballyturk with Larry's words stuffin' my body with butterflies – curtains start twitchin' and whispers start knittin' together until the air invisibly fills with Larry and me, me and Larry. The birds awaken from their fill of Cody's jumper and caw all manner of derision downwards – but all this carries me even higher! For there's passion and possibility in them hills – there's life above the grey of Ballyturk, surely!

1 (*distant*). Aren't you smellin'… lovely, Marnie?

   *2 turns and sees that* 1 *is by the flower – he's staring at it.*

2. Well that's awfully cheeky of ya, Ferdy Oppington!

   *2 waits for* 1 *to respond with a line.*

   *1, facing the wall, leans his head against it. He's exhausted/bewildered.*

   *2 is left to continue with the conversation himself – playing both parts.*

*Aren't you smellin' lovely, Marnie?* Well that's awfully cheeky of ya, Ferdy Oppington! *Where is it you're off ta, love?* I thought I might take a trip to the health centre and get myself a massage, actually. *There's a woman who does that down there, is there?* She's a form of woman, yes – by all accounts she wouldn't be the most feminine of women and yet she can reduce a seized back into a pound of putty in minutes!

*Suddenly 1 crashes his head against the wall.*

*Smellin' you right now, Marnie – and picturin' you bein' pounded by that She-Goliath – has sent my thoughts all a-skitter! I am aware of your emotional attachment to Larry Aspen…!* Are you though?! *I am!* Are you sure, Ferdy?

*A continuous high-pitched tone begins – low.*

*Your adhesion to that bedlamite is the most unnatural thing to surface in Ballyturk since that memorable afternoon when Clifford Cleary eloped with that pony! The whole town's sayin' it, Marnie – you deserve a better man!*

Take a hold of your faculties, Ferdy!

*1 has turned to look at 2 – his forehead's bleeding. The tone raising in volume –*

The mind is a thunderous place – with all manner of dreams and wants and half-notions and clouded thoughts. (*Beginning to shout.*) Look at you there – stood up by trousers and shirt – but inside – inside a calamitous vessel of frogs you are – a vessel adrift on a sea of thoughtless, unanswerable questions! Are you listening…?

*Suddenly a huge hydraulic noise – the sound of cracking.*

*Music.*

*The lights revert to the room's normal state as we watch the back wall slowly tear away from the two side walls.*

*Where it was joined to these walls – the wallpaper rips – power cables spark aggressively – water pipes buckle and spray water.*

*The two men stand frozen.*

*The wall continues opening and out into a beautiful blue
light – onto a small hill of green perfect grass – into what
must be the outside.*

*The wall falls onto this grass and we're looking at someone
standing on the hill.*

*As he looks up – the music swells.*

*He is a man in his sixties dressed in a darkish suit.*

*We'll call him* 3.

*He slowly walks towards the two men.*

*He steps into the room and the two men both take a step
backwards.*

*The music is gaining in volume and swirling now –* 1 *and* 2
*covering their ears to block the noise.*

3 *smokes.*

*Silence –* 1 *and* 2 *are stunned.*

*Then –*

3    (*about the cigarette*). Hope you don't mind. Terrible habit.
Been smokin' so long my right hand doesn't seem natural
without a cigarette in it. It seems undressed – a little bit
useless – or lazy – just hangin' there at the end of my wrist –
ageing a little bit faster than the rest of my body – so when
it's not functioning – when it's without a cigarette – it looks a
little idle and slackened. This hand – the left one – I'm less
critical of – I hardly think about it to be honest – I imagine
it's very happy that it was grown on the left side. It's got the
quieter existence of the two – a hand with pretty much little
functionality – it gets to laze about on desks and tables and
arms of chairs and legs of loved ones – and when it's brought
into life it's simply there to make shapes, to express, to dance
and ponce about. It must talk when it's holding the right hand
as it lies in bed at night and it must taunt the right hand about
havin' been dealt the easier hand, so to speak. How
exhausting to be writing and opening and turning and prising

and picking and poking and then the bloody wiping! – and then to be listening to my scorn almost every other hour because for all its action I am not in the least bit thankful to this right one because it's not of any use to me unless it's holding a cigarette as it is now! (*Slight pause*.) It seems unfair to focus and judge that which was born to work harder than the other one but which one has the fuller more colourful life but the right one, the doer of things… can I sit down?

*2 looks at 1.*

*They both walk quickly and set up the small table. There is some business as there's only two chairs.*

*2 scans the furniture for something approaching the right size to sit on as 3 and 1 sit at the table.*

*2 finds what looks like a metal safe. He begins to push it over to the table. This takes all his strength and a considerable time. 3 and 1 watch him bursting blood vessels (at one point he stops for a drink) and inching the safe closer and closer.*

*He finally gets to the table and sits on the safe.*

*A pause as the three just sit.*

Well this is nice! (*Slight pause. To 2.*) Do you have any tea?

2. We do yeah.

*A slight pause.*

3. Would you like to make some?

2. Not really no –

3. No you don't understand…

2. – it's not teatime yet! It will be soon and when that comes…

3. Make me a cup of tea.

2. Right.

3. Would you?

2. I'm thinking.

*A pause.*

Okay yeah.

3. Good man.

   *A pause as 3 stares at 2.*

2. You want me to make the tea now!?

3. Yes I'd like you to make me a cup of tea directly after I finish talking – make us all a cup of tea. That's three cups of teas I would like you to make in three separate cups. (*Slight pause.*) Finished.

   *2 hops up and walks towards the kitchen area.*

   And what d'you have for snacks!?

1. We have hot dogs.

2. We have biscuits with tea!

1. We also have biscuits that we have with our teas.

3. Fix us a selection of biscuits that we can dunk into our teas.

2. Right.

   *2 turns and gets to work.*

   *1 just stares at 3.*

   *3 turns to him. From his pocket he hands 1 a little scrap of toilet paper.*

   *1 wipes the blood from his forehead.*

3. You're much older than I thought you'd be, you know.

1. Really?

3. Yeah you are – much.

1. Oh.

   *A long pause.*

   *Then –*

3. People grow up fast – apparently that's a tragedy but I've never seen it that way myself because of the way things are with me. There are only ever two pictures – the face then and

the face now and it's interestin' to see what has stayed as is –
the eyes, the bones around the eyes, the chin – and what has
changed – what has been altered by wear and tear or by
familial strains – to grow into your parent's face – to be
pulled into the face of your father or mother and to follow as
they followed their parents' faces – to be led by the nose that
is no longer your nose but your father's nose, you get me?
Do you have mirrors here?

1. Just the one.

3. Well one's more than some and some don't even have
mirrors – so at least you've seen how you've aged – though
it's impossible to gauge that as time inches by – but you've
seen at least your reflection and maybe you notice small
changes weekly – have you?

1. What do you mean by 'weekly'?

*A slight pause.*

3. Look all you need to know is that you've got older – you're
no longer the you you were – and you are not yet the man
your father is – or was. D'you have hobbies?

1. We like to listen to music and dance. I like to draw things.

3. What things?

1. Whatever I see in my head.

*He gestures to his drawings on the walls.*

3. This – Ballyturk?

1. Yeah. All the people there, all their houses and the places they
shop – and the grey roads and the fields and woods and the
stream through town and the birds and cats and… everything.

*A slight pause.*

3. I collect things. That's what I'm here for.

*2 rushes over with three cups of tea and places them down.*

*He goes back to the kitchen and from a concealed area he
lifts up a selection of biscuits arranged into a massive
pyramid (three foot high).*

*2 carefully carries it over to the table and places the pyramid on the table. 3 is hidden behind it.*

*2 sits down on the metal safe with his own cup.*

*1 and 2 stare at the biscuits.*

*2 reaches out and inches a chocolate finger out of the pyramid (Jenga-style).*

*1 grabs a hold of a pink wafer and painstakingly eases it out. Success. He almost smiles when –*

*The pyramid collapses in a heap.*

*Suddenly a very loud muffled noise is heard behind the stage-left wall.*

Sshhhh!

*The old man from next door can be heard.*

VOICE 1. Well speaking personally – I never really trusted my body, do you know what I mean by that?

*The woman behind the other wall answers him –*

VOICE 3. Oh-God-yeah-absolutely-I-know-exactly-what-you-mean!

VOICE 1. I always felt my body was followin' me around sort of.

3. Like a stranger, d'you mean?

VOICE 1. More like a friend I had once been close to but am no longer.

3. Aye I see.

*1 and 2 are shocked that 3 can talk to them.*

VOICE 1. You do?

3. Absolutely I do. As a younger man my relationship with my body was a lot easier than it is now – sure now it's like walkin' about in an old suit.

VOICE 1. It's a terrible waster the body.

VOICE 3. It can eat food, mind you!

3. But sure it even discards that.

VOICE 1. Unless you're Fat-Grainne-Packer –

VOICE 3. – a woman who's yet to surrender to the motions of the bowel.

VOICE 1. It can be a useful form of transport – I'll give the body that.

3. In the early days it is.

VOICE 1. Exactly – in the early days.

3. Degradable is what the body is.

VOICE 1. Disembodiment is what I dream of.

3. Why can't the head give up?

VOICE 3. Because it's in competition to stay on top of the body!

VOICE 1. The head is a torturer!

3. Why not die?

VOICE 1. Sure isn't that what we're busy doin' here!?

VOICE 3. Life gets in the way – people say that.

3. Aye, people do say that.

VOICE 1. People are fond of sayin' all manner of…!

*A pause.*

*Blackout – for eight seconds –*

*Lights up with the alarm sounding and 1 and 2 wake up and hop out of their bed – the table, safe and chairs are gone.*

*They look at 3 who is already walking towards the alarm clock, eating a Marietta biscuit.*

*He finds the golf club leaning against the wall.*

*He places the clock on the floor and looks down at it screaming up at him.*

*With the golf club he lines up his shot.* 1 *and* 2 *slowly step out of the way.*

*As* 3 *draws back the club – the alarm suddenly cuts.*

*The jazz classic 'Time After Time' (Cahn/Styne; Chet Baker's version) plays warmly in the space.*

3 *begins to sing the first few lines of 'Time After Time' through the golf club.*

*He then sees something on the floor beneath him.*

*He sings another couple of lines.*

*He bends down and picks up the dead fly and holds it in his hand.*

*He sings another line.*

*He gently closes his hand.*

*He sings another few lines.*

*He raises his hand to his own ear – the sound of the fly buzzing loudly as it drowns out and cuts 'Time After Time'.*

*It's come back to life.*

3 *lowers his hand and lets the fly free.*

*Then –*

3. I wonder do they know how brief their life will be? You know, whether it's somethin' they're thinking about as they grow inside that shell of theirs – is it somethin' they can ever imagine? Is it passed down from their parents and lies inside them – and those broken images of the outside world passed down also and grown over those days as they grow inside. And they can hear surely the world outside – the incredible sounds – and how do they match what little they know with what actually is? What version of life are they making up inside those little homes? And maybe that's why the fly arrives out so noisy and feverish – it joins his brothers and sisters and they fly in hordes to start with – but the world they see is so much larger and quickly they're led by the instinct, by the breeze, by the need to discover things

alone, by the knowledge that their time is so short. Outside and flying over and through something that seemingly has no order 'cause all is textures to them up there. There's a breeze that holds them and underneath is grass or maybe sand or rock turned into road – and there's peculiar-shaped bushes and trees – and each tree singular – each with its own needs, its own particular life – and yet all wanting to commune with other plants or animals – wanting to populate the world with its particular shape and colour and kind. From one season to the next a million flies grow from just a few and they fly over a landscape itself competing for more life, for time, for legacy. (*Slight pause*.) Did ya give each other names by the way?

*The flies noisily disappear.*

1. No.

3. And why not?

1. I don't know why.

3  (*to* 2). Can't ya remember deciding that?

2. No.

3. Did ya know I would come back?

*A slight pause.*

2. Maybe once I did.

3. But you'd forgotten. Everyone does. Everyone does.

*He looks at 1's drawings on the wall. He then calls him over.*

*1 goes to him and 3 faces him in front of the wall.*

*2 stands on the far side of the stage, isolated.*

What do you see when you speak about Ballyturk – do you imagine people's faces and homes – can you see them?

1. I see him as them – I see the drawings as the places – sometimes I see nothing but the word.

3. Because none of it's real – before the fly, before me.

1. Only inside our heads it is.

3. And that's enough for you?

1. I don't understand what you're asking.

3. Right.

*A pause. Then –*

Everything you've imagined – it is. All life. It's out there. Everything.

*Like a light has gone off in him – 3 visibly fades. He looks spent – older now.*

*He looks over at the flower on the shelf. He opens the top drawer in the chest drawer and takes out the knife.*

*He goes to the marigold and quickly slices at the stem but it remains standing.*

*He fires the knife into the top of the chest of drawers.*

*He carefully picks the marigold off the stem – he's cut it beautifully.*

*He places the marigold in the buttonhole of his jacket.*

*He begins – maybe talking to himself –*

There's a man and he wakes alone. His eyes open and he's conscious of his first breath, of his first movement, of his first thought which may be of food or may be to shuffle himself to his bathroom and relieve himself. And those first beginnings lie on top of twenty-three thousand mornings that have passed where he has aged invisibly, definitely – where he carries half-remembered bits of his life, of the people he has met and hated and loved, of his brothers and sisters who were once his world and now only exist to make him feel older. He carries a billion pictures of life that have no consequence to him and a few pictures which will always haunt or please him. He's made from purpose and mistake and controlled by the movement of this planet around a star – yet in the second he's led by some great need or some little urgency. Only occasionally he's conscious that around him life is beginning and ending to the beat of time – that millions of others are walking in the exact same moment that he is – are travelling with the same purpose but with singular histories – but travelling nonetheless with the same basic need – to keep on living. How unremarkable and how faintly unique to wake and walk in this way – with doors pushing open into a sky bizarrely blue and giving to us systems of weather, shaping us with forever-movable seasons. And too hard it is to think how rain is made – how the sun can push light through darkness – and what it is that holds us up here imperceptibly in space – that man stands and walks in life as it is now – with geographies to navigate – with journeys to his wife, to his work, to lunches, to beaches, to churches, to secret meetings with potential lovers, to parks, to other parts of the village, or town, or city, or countries even. A lifetime of walking distances in the vain hope of making things that bit more fulfilling – of packing his time with experiences some of which will change him greatly and others with no consequence other than wasting a little more of his life. And to stand there in the magnificence of this world with all these animals and plants and trees too many to ever imagine clearly – and standing with the you as was made – in a life that is so chaotically structured by nature – to continue living – to remain upright and to be able to carry on searching for something other than what you have – some love or money or experience or cat or cake or son or anything at all – something which makes you continue without the mindfulness of it all ending at any moment – for everything is here and we are here to lay down legacy – to give life purpose by reaching its edge. (*Slight pause*.) And it's time for you two and for what you've made – time for one of you to walk away and into your passing. In leaving you're giving shape to life – some design and purpose for being what you are – for this is the order that all life demands – (*Slight pause*.) it needs a death.

*A long pause.*

3 *is finished.*

*Then –*

I can't see the start of my life to figure out how I've come to this... this work. (*Slight pause.*) You give me a choice of biscuits – I give you a choice as to which one of you will step outside, walk the twelve seconds to me and die.

*He takes his packet of cigarettes from his jacket pocket. There's one left.*

It's all been said. By me, at least. (*Slight pause.*) Right.

*The music he enters to – returns now.*

*He turns around and walks out of the room and onto the grassy hill outside.*

*He stands there and the warm sun catches his face in profile as he places the cigarette in his mouth.*

*The wall rises noisily back up.*

*It crashes back into position – the music cutting abruptly.*

*The two men locked inside their room once more – turn and look at each other.*

*Then –*

*– the turntable begins to spin again, the arm and needle moving into position and onto the record.*

*They stand across the space listening to the needle crackling on the vinyl – waiting and expecting Blancmange to play once again.*

*Suddenly Yazoo launches into 'Situation'.*

*On 0:10 the two men race in opposite directions. They rifle through a chest of drawers full of marbles and table-tennis balls – that scatter across the floor.*

*They both find a skipping rope on 0:20.*

*On 0:25 they both begin to skip like professional boxers.*

*On 0:34 they throw their skipping ropes to the side.*

*2 takes off his shirt, grabs some suspension flexible cables attached to the left wall and begins some vigorous suspension training.*

*Meanwhile on the right wall, 1 has wrapped a canvas belt around his backside. He pushes a button and it begins to vibrate while he brushes his teeth.*

*On 1:02, 1 gets out of his vibrating belt, takes off his T-shirt and begins his own suspension training – while 2 has finished his and gets on an old stationary cycle machine (bolted to the wall) and cycles fast. As 2 cycles he's peeling mandarins and popping them in his mouth.*

*On 1:25, 2 races over and gets into the vibrating belt as 1 gets on the cycling machine.*

*All this time and their minds are racing with what 3 has left in the room – perhaps the exercise will expel these thoughts of life and death.*

*On 1:47 the two men finish their exercise.*

*1 grabs two spray-on deodorants from the right wall and 2 grabs two Remington electric razors from the left wall. They look across the space and suddenly race towards each other.*

*The deodorants and electric razors are attached to super-resistant elastic cables.*

*The two men just about meet in the middle where 2 shaves 1 and 1 deodorises 2 – in this manner they spring back and forth from their walls until –*

*– at 2:23 they and Yazoo stop.*

2. So to finish what I started earlier – it's impossible to second-guess what hair will do – and although it gives me great pleasure – it's living and dying at a ferocious rate – it's an awful shame that some are regarded as hair solely.

1. Like Lexy Stafford.

2. A pioneer who polishes his crown as much as he does his boots – a man whose head caught fire on All Souls' Day and was eventually put out on Christmas Eve.

1. Honey Chasty.

2. A badly named glutton of a woman whose matted hair sat in the corner of The Rusty Anchor smelling of cheese and groaning.

1. Little-Mick Langley.

2. A balding midget who roamed Delaney's Field looking like a friendless football in winter.

*The cuckoo clock suddenly sounds. Saved by the bird and 2 is already heading for the darts.*

Hair's a cunning temptress all right – more often than not I feel like a fool to the follicle.

*2 opens the curtain –*

*– the Ballyturk sign barely flickers on.*

*2 throws the three darts quickly in succession.*

*He quickly cranks the lever – grabs 1 and throws him into the spotlight.*

Do it!

*Then –*

1. I'm too scared to talk.

2. Then don't.

*1 pulls the lever back and the space is lit back up.*

Go on.

*A pause.*

1. Bits and pieces of the almost forgotten – pictures I thought that were stolen from Ballyturk – where before they could never have been mine – now that man's face is knittin' them all together. What must be sand is on a seat – what must be the sun is shining through a window – and a small jaw chewing something sticky – of teeth almost being pulled from gums and fingers passing over the seat and through the sand – and bare feet dusted too and a body not yet broken by this room – it sits all happy in the back of a car – it's made still from what was before, by the sun, by the running, by the

'beach' is the word – and moments from sleep were it not for this sugar being chewed into my mouth. My mouth. (*Slight pause*.) It was mine. (*Slight pause*.) And I'm not in Ballyturk, not in any place we made – beyond the car window all is bleached by this light – there must be a street or shops out there – there could be car noises or sounds of the real countryside even. The light buckles and his face looking in at me – and I'm no longer there with the sun but somewhere else – and moving fast with him driving in front – and what could have been trees and what might have been real clouds – and what certainly is colour is passing me with that man's voice telling me to be quiet! Did he bring me here – was it him?!

2. I can't be sure…

1. You know it was him!

2. Maybe it was…

1. And there was a door I came through…

2. It doesn't open.

1. There's an actual door?!

2. Of course there is…

1. And where is it!?

2. It was easier not seeing the door…

1. Do you know my name?

2. I made myself forget it.

1. Why would you do that!?

2. I don't know why…

1. Do you know your name?

2. None of that's important…!

> 1 *suddenly collapses on the ground and convulses violently.*
>
> *After ten seconds he stops.*
>
> *Then –*

We don't cry here – we said that once.

1. I know we don't.

*A long pause as 2 stands and looks down at him.*

*Then –*

2. There was nothing to start with – and out of that me and you pushed words. (*Slight pause*.) 'Above and there's large clouds looking like islands and through them sunlight shines down – and down on a small town lying by these woods on a hill.' Twenty-seven words I used first.

*A pause.*

1. 'And in the woods birds caw all manner of noise and drown out the stream that runs through the trees –

*As they construct Ballyturk – quiet sounds accompany them.*

– and out slowly the stream moves through the town as Ballyturk wakes.'

2. 'And flat terraced houses stand by flat terraced shops – three narrow roads drawn with tarmac and battered by time and rain.'

1. 'And the people of Ballyturk sit on their beds – morning light and radio sounds placing them up and pushing doors and standing out on Moyne Street in clothes stuck with damp and country air. They start.'

*During the below the Ballyturk lighting begins to fade back in.*

2. And it's Jankie Roller –

1. – and Larry Aspen –

2. – and Cody Finnington –

1. – and Ferdy Oppinton –

2. – and each with their own wants, each with their own skin and voice and each shaped differently – each pushin' their doors open into what's been knitted by us.

*The sound of the shop door 'dinging' open.*

Hello there, Mrs Drench.

*Shattered and 1 can't answer.*

*Again the sound of the shop door 'dinging' open.*

 Hello there, Mrs Drench.

*Automatically and 1 slowly walks to the wall and climbs to the high shelf.*

*Then –*

1. Oh hello there, Ferdy. Aren't you lookin' smart for pullin' pints in The Rusty Anchor tonight.

2. Pullin' a kiss from Marnie Reynolds, I hope.

1. And drivin' Larry Aspen green so. Terrible temper on that man – we'll know where that temper will end, Ferdy. In badness, I'd imagine.

   *A slight pause.*

2. I wondered whether you had any lemons, Mrs Drench?

1. I haven't seen a lemon in well over a year I'd say.

2. Oh. And why's that?

1. I won't be out-bittered by a lemon, Ferdy.

2. Bye-bye then.

   *1 listens to the detailed sounds of Moyne Street all around them now.*

   *Then –*

1. Who's making these sounds?

   *The sounds suddenly stop.*

   *A pause.*

2. I'll go to him. It should be me. The eldest should die first.

   *A slight pause.*

1. And what do I do?

   *A slight pause.*

2. Live.

*On the floor the alarm clock suddenly starts to sound.*

*Lights snap to previous as 2 rushes towards it and starts stamping on it.*

*Suddenly the record player switches itself on and the intro to 'Dancing with Tears in My Eyes' by Ultravox blasts out.*

*1 goes to the record player, rips up the single and fires it across the space. As it hits the stage-right wall, Nena's '99 Red Balloons' begins to play.*

*1 flicks through the records and finds that single and flings it at the wall – as it smashes, Survivor's 'Eye of the Tiger' starts to play.*

*1 flicks through the records and finds it. Furious – he grabs a handful of records and starts smashing them against the stage right wall – unleashing more snippets of eighties classics.*

*The four voices on either side of them are heard – the words from their previous scenes are heard clearly, then spun backwards and distorted.*

*The pathetic shower suddenly turns itself on – the cuckoo starts firing in and out of the clock.*

*2 still can't get the alarm off. He's punched it, removed its innards, swallowed bits of it – but still it's blasting and getting even louder.*

*Blackout but the noise and music continues.*

*After four seconds the lights pop back up and 2 jumps out of the bed.*

*The back wall jolts open two foot and daylight streaks through.*

*2 looks over at 1 being driven mad by these records/by everything.*

*But this alarm is still sounding.*

*2 gathers up all the pieces of the alarm clock and throws them in the microwave and puts it on.*

*He steps back. The microwave explodes.*

*1 flings the last record at the wall – Rick Astley's 'Together Forever' – it shatters and all sounds immediately cut.*

*Silence.*

*Suddenly the cuckoo clock noisily goes on fire.*

*1 walks slowly towards it – dazed/terrified.*

*2 has rushed to a press and takes out a fire extinguisher. He returns fast to put the fire out but 1 is standing in the way blocking him.*

1. Let it burn – I can't go on…

   *2 fires up the extinguisher, blasting it at the clock and putting out the fire.*

   What is this place!?

2  (*shutting off the fire extinguisher*). Our home.

1. It's not what it was – it's never been what it was…!

2. You'll learn to forget – we did before.

1. A child could forget but not me now!

   *A slight pause.*

2  (*quietly*). I can't let you die – I won't do that.

1. One walks and one stays talking but either way it's the same death.

   *2 smashes 1 in the face, grabs him by the back of the head and talks clearly to him –*

2. I'll walk those twelve seconds to him and each step I'll know that you're in here breathing – that'll be all the life I need – d'you understand?

1. Yeah.

   *A slight pause.*

   Or I think I do – I don't know.

1 *lowers his head.* 2 *looks at him.*

1 *pulls the knife out of the top of the chest of drawers.*

*Then –*

There must have been more thoughts on that first day I spent here? Thoughts of parents and maybe brothers and sisters – of another place I lived – a house, a room where I slept and drew pictures – and those memories would have followed me around and outlasted my crying – and maybe I even talked about them – and you of your life as a boy – of course you talked. Maybe you still remembered your life. And we'd listen to each other and time passes quickly and the detail of before, the bad feelings first they fade of course – everything's eaten by the now – by what we build, by what we've become – all this life where Ballyturk appears out of the darkness and we enter that town as other people shaped from half-ideas – their houses and streets and trees willed into life to push us further from what we knew in our stomachs was real life behind that wall. (*Slight pause.*) How can I stay here knowing what there is there? How can I talk about Ballyturk knowing that it's only ever inside this breaking body and nowhere else? There's no freedom to it – it's filling rooms with words, not real life… so how?

*A pause. He turns and looks at 2 and how broken he looks.*

For you I'll stay – 'cause you're more than myself – whatever that might be. I'll stay.

1 *stares over at his drawings.*

*A pause.*

*A sudden thought –*

And maybe knit these words you taught me into something brand new. Walk us both together in words as the one person. The wall opens to the outside –

*He places the knife on the table and turns 2 towards his drawings and stands behind him.*

*Music.*

– and with your back to me you walk the twelve seconds it
takes to reach him. You walk over the grass and you're a part
of a world full of journeys, the to and fro of small adventure,
of ever-changing pictures and people. There's a stillness in
the breeze out there but each ounce of life is altered by you
now walking in it – you, passed through the air and out over
countryside, over what must be oceans and part of the
texture of real life now. You're there in the grass and
stretched out in trees and made alive by day and spun in
colours too heartbreaking to mention. Land and sea holding
each other and holding upon it these people carried along by
heartbeat and dreams of love and talking to one another and
waking with one another and planning uncertain futures that
are free, that have possibility as you do now in these twelve
seconds that you walk –

1 *covers his own eyes and really tries to be there.*

– and each step walked away from what was taken from us,
what was wasted and stolen by something other than us –
and a step right now brings chance, a breath can fill with
hope, where a boy can feel the sun on his face and throw
open a door and run in a day dusted in not just the word
'beach' but the beach itself – while another boy walks in a
countryside forever free and talking endlessly to a sister –
talking stupidly.

2 *turns to look at him.*

You walk from this room and your spirit, past and present,
wraps with the spirit of billions of others, and it's this that
invisibly holds up this planet of ours in space – in brilliant
openness – in freedom. You walk away quietly.

1 *lowers his hands and sees* 2 *looking at him.*

And it must be happiness you feel – and what you're
walking towards is forgotten – or if remembered it holds no
fear this 'death'. (*Slight pause.*) You're a lived person and in
those twelve seconds you're a part of the world – you've
stared at a life and walked in it and it's all the life you need.
It's real. Real life.

*Suddenly the wall begins to open out – but this time there is no mechanical noise –*

*– it is the imagined quiet elemental sounds of the Earth heard from our troposphere – of winds, oceans, nature, of us.*

*The wall opens and the evening light is beautiful out there – and on the small hill, little marigold flowers have grown in the grass.*

*1 and 2 look towards it.*

*On the hill and 3 is seated behind an office desk, waiting for his dead.*

*The wall lands softly on the grass.*

*Then –*

2.  Go on.

    *For a beat – 1 is unsure what's been said.*

    Go.

    *1 turns away and walks from the room and into life.*

    *It's 2 who stays. He covers his eyes.*

    *1 walks in the outside through the world – for twelve seconds he's free.*

    *3 stands up from his seat to meet him.*

    *The wall rises again.*

    *All sounds cut as the wall closes and shuts 2 back into the room.*

    *He takes his hands away from his eyes and stands alone in the silence for some moments.*

    *He doesn't know what to do.*

    *He slowly turns around and looks at his cell.*

    *He stares at 1's drawings on the walls. He walks closer and closer to the stage-left wall – and stops a foot away from a drawing.*

*The cuckoo clock sounds three times. He turns and looks blankly at it.*

*Suddenly there's a knocking from the stage-right wall. Instinctively 2 picks up the knife from the table.*

*The knocking more desperate now as 2 walks towards a chest of drawers. It's coming from behind there.*

*In one movement he moves back the furniture fast.*

*Behind there the wall is moving – a small door has been wallpapered over – someone is trying to get in.*

*2 quickly shoves the knife into the wall and cuts around the door – which reaches four foot in height.*

*He stops and stands back.*

*Very slowly the door opens inwards.*

*A long pause.*

*A seven-year-old* GIRL *enters dressed in leggings, runners and a sweatshirt.*

*Lost and frightened she stares at 2 – expecting him to hurt her.*

*Music.*

*Behind her the little door closes shut.*

*Feeling no threat from 2 – the* GIRL *turns and looks at the room as the music swells.*

*2 turns and looks out.*

*His eyes slowly close.*

*Blackout.*

*The End – the music continuing in darkness.*